THE DIABETIC COOKBOOK AFTER 50

Easy Low-Sugar and Low-Fat Recipes for a Healthy Lifestyle Over 50

By

Taste Books

Table of Contents

INTRODUCTION 1
Things To Know About Diabetes 3
    What is Diabetes? 3
    Types of Diabetes 4
    Diabetes In People Over 50 5
    What Is Glycemic Index? 8
    Blood Sugar Levels in Diabetes 10
    Various Tests for Blood Sugar Levels 11
Chapter 1 12
Treat Diabetes with Diet and Exercise 12
    What Is the Most Effective Diabetic Diet Plan? 12
    General Diet Guide: 15
    Foods Permitted and Foods to Avoid 15
    Making a Diet Plan 17
    Exercise in Diabetes Management 19
Chapter 2: 22
4-Week Meal Plan 22
Chapter 3: 26
Breakfast Recipes 26
Avocado Toast with Poached Egg 27
Greek Yogurt Parfait 27
Spinach and Mushroom Breakfast Wrap 28
Veggie Omelet 28
Whole Grain Pancakes 29
Chapter 4: 30
Snack and Side 30
Greek Yogurt with Berries 31
Baked Sweet Potato Fries 31
Veggie Sticks with Hummus 32
Caprese Skewers 32
Baked Kale Chips 33
Cottage Cheese and Tomato Salad 33
Quick Lemon-Blueberry Bites 34
Guacamole with Veggie Slices 35
Baked Zucchini Chips 35
Deviled Eggs 36

Apple Slices with Peanut Butter 36
Roasted Chickpeas 37
Cucumber and Smoked Salmon Roll-Ups 37
Baked Parmesan Zucchini Fries 38
Turkey Lettuce Wraps 38
Baked Eggplant Chips 39
Spicy Roasted Edamame 39
Baked Buffalo Cauliflower Bites 40
Mini Bell Pepper Nachos 40
Roasted Honeynut Squash 41
Chapter 5: **42**
Soups and Salad 42
Mixed Greens Salad with Grilled Chicken 43
Lentil Soup 43
Spinach and Berry Salad 44
Tomato Basil Soup 44
Quinoa and Vegetable Salad 45
Chicken Vegetable Soup 45
Greek Salad 46
Minestrone Soup 46
Tuna Salad with Avocado 47
Butternut Squash Soup 47
Roasted Beet and Orange Salad 48
Spinach and Feta Soup 48
Kale and Chickpea Soup 49
Mexican Quinoa Salad 49
Chicken Tortilla Soup 50
Chapter 6: **51**
Fish and Sea Food 51
Baked Lemon Herb Salmon 52
Grilled Shrimp Skewers 52
Lemon Garlic Baked Salmon 53
Tuna Salad Lettuce Wraps 53
Baked White Fish with Tomatoes and Olives 54
Grilled Salmon with Avocado Salsa 54
Garlic and Herb Baked Shrimp 55
Seared Scallops with Cauliflower Mash 55
Baked Lemon Dijon Tilapia 56
Grilled Lemon Herb Swordfish 56
Steamed Asian Ginger White Fish 57
Grilled Lemon Garlic Halibut 57
Blackened Cajun Shrimp Salad 58

Baked Dijon Salmon 59
Broiled Lemon Garlic Swordfish...59
Thai Coconut Curry Shrimp 60
Greek Style Baked White Fish...61
Lemon Pepper Grilled Tuna Steaks 61
Pesto Shrimp with Zucchini Noodles 62
Baked Parmesan Crusted Haddock..62
Shrimp and Avocado Salad 63

Chapter 7: 64

Poultry and Meat 64
Grilled Lemon Herb Chicken 65
Turkey Meatballs with Zucchini Noodles......................................65
Herb-Roasted Chicken Breast with Vegetables 66
Grilled Herb-Marinated Turkey Tenderloin 66
Grilled Teriyaki Chicken Stir-Fry 67
Oven-Roasted Turkey Breast..67
Grilled Balsamic Glazed Pork Chops 68
Herb-Crusted Baked Chicken Thighs 68
Chicken and Broccoli Stir-Fry 69

Chapter 8: 70

Desserts and Drinks..70
Sugar-Free Apple Crisp 71
Chocolate Avocado Mousse 71
Low-Carb Berry Chia Pudding 72
Sugar-Free Banana Bread..72
Greek Yogurt Parfait 73
Cinnamon Pear Crumble 73
Sugar-Free Coconut Macaroons 74
Coconut Chia Seed Popsicles 74
Iced Green Tea with Lemon and Mint 75
Sparkling Berry Infused Water 75
Pumpkin Spice Smoothie...76
Almond Flour Blueberry Muffins..76
Cucumber Mint Cooler 77

Chapter 9: 78

Meatless Main Dishes 78
Lentil and Vegetable Stir-Fry..79
Vegetable Stir-Fry..79
Eggplant Parmesan 80
Chickpea Curry..80
Quinoa Stuffed Bell Peppers 81
Lentil and Vegetable Casserole 82

Spinach and Chickpea Curry 83
Spinach and Feta Stuffed Portobello Mushrooms 84
Tofu and Vegetable Stir-Fry 84
Zucchini Noodles with Tomato and Basil 85
Black Bean and Vegetable Enchiladas 85
Cauliflower Fried Rice 86
Lentil and Sweet Potato Curry 86
Caprese Stuffed Portobello Mushrooms 87
Sweet Potato and Black Bean Chili 87
Mediterranean Quinoa Salad 88
Lentil and Vegetable Soup 88
Spinach and Mushroom Quiche 89
Chickpea and Vegetable Curry 89
Vibrant Green Carbonara 90
Veggie Stir-Fry with Tofu 90
Putting Your Healthy Shopping List Together 91
List Of Recipes in Alphabetical Order with Page Number 93
REFERENCES **97**

INTRODUCTION

In today's fast-paced world, where unhealthy food options abound, and sedentary lifestyles have become the norm, you face unique challenges in managing your health and well-being as you enter your golden years. But fret not because this book is here to lend a helping hand.

The milestone of 50 years represents a wonderful period of experience, wisdom, and self-discovery. However, it is also a time when our bodies naturally go through changes, such as changes in metabolism, hormonal changes, and a higher chance of developing chronic illnesses like diabetes. Therefore, it is vital to comprehend these changes and adjust to them, and one of the best ways to do this is by consuming a healthy, balanced diet.

This cookbook has been carefully designed to meet the special dietary requirements of people with diabetes who are 50 years of age or older. It is a priceless resource that provides a wealth of nutritional knowledge, useful advice, and a tempting selection of delectable recipes that put taste, health, and simplicity of preparation first.

You will embark on a life-changing culinary trip via the pages of this cookbook, learning how to properly fuel your body and mind while controlling your blood sugar levels. We are aware that managing diabetes necessitates paying close attention to what we eat, but we are adamant that flavor or enjoyment should never be sacrificed for good nutrition.

The Cookbook for a Diabetic Diet encourages you to see meals as a chance to relish bright flavors, embrace nourishment, and celebrate your well-being. Each dish is carefully crafted, taking into account the dietary demands of people managing diabetes, focusing on the requirements and difficulties faced after age 50.

This book offers a variety of recipes for everything from breakfast to dinner, snacks to desserts, and everything in between, drawing on the knowledge of nutritionists, dieticians, and culinary experts. You can choose from a delectable variety of dishes, from savory classics to cutting-edge culinary inventions, to make sure that your meals are not only delicious but also include the ideal proportion of vital nutrients.

information on portion control, carbohydrate counting, and useful advice for keeping blood sugar levels steady. We recognize that managing diabetes can occasionally feel daunting, but this guide is here to provide support, inspiration, and a wealth of knowledge backed by science to help you on your path.

The Diabetic Diet Cookbook After 50 is a companion created to enrich your life, improve your culinary experiences, and motivate you to take charge of your health whether you have diabetes for the first time or have had it for a long time. This book attempts to promote a healthy connection with food, fostering well-being, vigor, and the self-assurance to live life to the fullest via the power of nutrition and mindful eating.

Consequently, let's set out on this amazing journey together, where each meal narrates a tale of health, hope, and the pleasure of feeding our bodies after age 50. To turn managing diabetes into an educational and delectable adventure, open these pages, awaken your taste buds, and set off on a culinary exploration journey.

Things To Know About Diabetes

What is Diabetes?

Hyperglycemia also known as diabetes is a chronic metabolic disease characterized by high blood glucose levels. This happens when there is insufficient insulin production or the body can't function effectively as an insulin producer. Insulin is the hormone made by the pancreas, which controls glucose's uptake and use in the body. A worldwide standard definition of diabetes is set by the American Diabetes Association ADA. According to the ADA:

" The disease is characterized by high blood glucose levels because of abnormalities in the body's ability to produce and use insulin. The body doesn't produce insulin when it is type 1 diabetes. The body does not produce enough insulin in type 2 diabetes, the most commonly occurring kind of diabetes. Some people with type 2 diabetes may also produce little to no insulin."

A definition by the American Diabetes Association includes diabetes as a group of diseases with elevated blood sugar levels caused by deficiencies in insulin production and management. Insulin, as you have already noted, is the hormone that plays a major role in controlling blood sugar levels.
Type 1 and type 2 diabetes have been distinguished from each other in the definition. Due to the autoimmune response that deletes insulin producing cells within the pancreas, type 1 diabetes can't be produced by the body. As a result, people with type 1 diabetes will require insulin therapy for the rest of their lives to regulate their blood glucose levels.

By contrast, type 2 diabetes occurs when the body is resistant to insulin's effects or does not correctly use insulin. In type 2 diabetes, the pancreas may still produce insulin, but the body's cells cannot efficiently utilize it. This insulin resistance leads to elevated blood sugar levels. It is important to note that the pancreas may also decrease insulin production in some cases of type 2 diabetes.

Overall, the ADA definition of diabetes encompasses the concepts of high blood glucose levels, defects in insulin production or utilization, and the distinction between type 1 and type 2 diabetes. This definition helps to understand the fundamental mechanisms underlying diabetes and the need for appropriate management strategies tailored to each type.

In the same vein, the National Institute of Diabetes and Digestive and Kidney Diseases (NIDDK) also provides an acceptable definition well recognized by medical practitioners as thus:

"Diabetes is a disease that occurs when your blood glucose, also called blood sugar, is too high. You get most of your energy from blood glucose, which is found in foods you eat. Insulin, a hormone that is produced by the pancreas, helps glucose from food enter cells and be used for energy."

Diabetic disease is described by NIDDK definition as a condition characterized by elevated glucose levels in the blood. It is stated that the primary energy source on our body comes from blood glucose derived from food. In diabetes, blood glucose regulation is disrupted, leading to chronically high levels. Insulin, a hormone produced by the pancreas, plays a crucial role in facilitating the entry of glucose into food into cells for energy. In diabetes, either insufficient insulin is produced or the body becomes resistant to its effects, resulting in impaired glucose utilization and high blood sugar levels.

Both definitions emphasize the role of insulin and the impact of elevated blood sugar levels on various bodily systems. In addition, they provide a clear understanding of diabetes as a chronic condition characterized by dysregulated blood sugar and the importance of managing it to prevent complications.

Types of Diabetes

Diabetes is a metabolic disorder that develops when the pancreas is unable to produce enough insulin for your body to normally convert the sugars you consume into energy. Diabetes comes in three main varieties.

Diabetes Type 1.

This particular form of diabetes is an autoimmune disorder, which develops when the body is unable to combat an infection effectively. The outcome is that the body starts attacking its own cells, in this instance, the beta cells in the pancreas that make insulin. Because the body destroys the beta cells, no insulin is made. Therefore, type 1 diabetes requires daily insulin injections to live.

Although the exact origins of type-1 diabetes are unknown, autoimmune, genetic, and environmental factors are thought to contribute to its development. Anyone can get it, but it is more common in children and adolescents. Increased thirst and urination, continuous hunger, blurred vision, unexplained weight loss, and weariness are all signs of type 1 diabetes. Therefore, it's crucial to get a type-1 diabetes diagnosis as soon as possible. A person with this kind of diabetes faces a high risk of slipping into a diabetic coma, a potentially fatal condition, without receiving daily insulin injections.

Diabetes Type 2.

The most prevalent form of diabetes is this one. Adults with type-2 diabetes are typically obese, have a family history of the disease, or have experienced gestational diabetes in the past. Type-2 diabetes isn't brought on by the body's inability to make insulin; rather, it's brought on by the body's inability to effectively use the insulin it produces. Because of this, the blood sugar levels are elevated.

Frequent thirst and urination, nausea, unexplained weight loss, recurrent infections, sluggish wound, and sore healing, and exhaustion are all signs of type 2 diabetes.

A nutritious diet and regular exercise are just two examples of lifestyle adjustments that can frequently avoid or control this kind of diabetes. To successfully manage the symptoms of type-2 diabetes, some individuals must take pharmaceuticals, while many others turn to alternative remedies.

Gestational Diabetes.

This form of diabetes affects expectant mothers and is brought on by a sensitivity to carbs, which raises blood sugar levels. To avoid the baby being harmed at birth, it is crucial for a woman with gestational diabetes to manage her condition. There is a chance that the baby could be born with insulin shock if the pregnant woman's blood sugar levels are not under control.

Risk factors for gestational diabetes include obesity, advanced maternal age, and a family history of diabetes. Although gestational diabetes symptoms typically go away after delivery, both the mother and the baby are in serious danger. The mother is more likely to get type-2 diabetes subsequently, and the child is more likely to grow up to be obese or have diabetes.

Stopping the Development of Diabetes.

Diabetes is frequently preventable, or development can be postponed. A change in lifestyle can effectively control all three forms of diabetes. The most significant adjustment is a healthy diet because eating nutritious foods regularly enables your body to carry out the functions required for survival. Fresh produce, fiber, and Omega-3 fatty acids should all be abundant in a healthy diet. After receiving a diabetes diagnosis of any kind, a person should closely monitor their carbohydrate intake and drastically cut back on their sugar intake.

Your general health benefits from regular exercise. Maintaining healthy blood flow and toned muscles will help your body function as it should. This will enable your body to carry out its typical functions.

In order to prevent more serious illnesses and diseases that can be related to diabetes, such as heart disease and stroke, it is crucial for early diagnosis and proper treatment of the condition. Although diabetics are more likely to get various diseases and conditions, it's crucial to remember that taking care of your health will take care of you.

Diabetes In People Over 50

Although diabetes can afflict persons of any age, it is most common in those over 50. The prevalence, risk factors, complications, management, and preventative strategies of diabetes in this age group will all be covered in this debate.

Prevalence

Diabetes is more common as people age, and this trend is more pronounced in those over 50. The International Diabetes Federation estimates that 20% of adults in this age range globally have diabetes. This can be due to several variables, including aging-related changes in the body's ability to produce and use insulin, a higher risk of acquiring other chronic health issues, and lifestyle elements such as poor diet and inactivity.

Risk elements

In people over 50, diabetes can develop due to a number of risk factors. These consist of the following:

- **Age:** Diabetes is significantly more likely to develop as people age. People are more likely to develop diabetes as they age because of a loss in pancreatic function and insulin sensitivity.

- **Family History:** A person's risk of developing type 2 diabetes is increased by having a close relative with the disease.

- **Sedentary Lifestyle:** Diabetes is more likely to develop in those with sedentary lifestyles who don't engage in regular physical activity. Regular exercise aids in maintaining a healthy weight and improving insulin sensitivity.

- **Unhealthy Diet:** Diabetes can be facilitated by poor dietary decisions, such as a high intake of processed meals, sugary drinks, and a deficiency in fruits and vegetables.

Complications

Diabetes can lead to a number of problems, and people over the age of 50 are at a higher risk for these problems. Some such issues include:

- **Cardiovascular disease:** Diabetes raises cardiovascular disease risk, including heart attack, stroke, and coronary artery disease. Because of the combined effects of vascular disease brought on by diabetes and age-related changes, this risk is particularly severe in older people.

- **Kidney disease:** Diabetes is a major contributor to chronic kidney disease. Diabetes increases the chance of developing diabetic nephropathy in older people, which can lead to kidney failure.

- **Diabetic retinopathy:** There is a complication of diabetes that affects blood vessels in the eye called diabetic retinopathy which can result in diabetic retinopathy and potentially loss of vision. This risk may significantly impact the quality of life for older people, which rises with age.

Management

The treatment of diabetes in adults over 50 requires a multifaceted strategy that includes dietary changes, medication, and routine monitoring. Key elements in managing diabetes include:

- **Diet and exercise:** Maintaining healthy blood sugar levels can be achieved by eating a diet high in whole grains, fruits, vegetables, and lean proteins. Regular exercise, such as brisk walking or aerobics, is crucial for managing diabetes and preserving general health.

- **Medication:** Depending on the type and degree of diabetes, medicinal products may be used to control blood sugar levels. Injections of insulin or oral anti-diabetic drugs may be used. Due to age-related changes in metabolism and possible interactions with other medications, they may be taking, older people may need to increase their medication dosages.

- **Regular Monitoring:** For effective diabetic management, regular blood glucose monitoring is essential. This may entail utilizing a glucometer or continuous glucose monitoring equipment for self-monitoring blood glucose levels.

Preventive Actions

Many preventive steps can be performed to lessen the chance of getting the condition, even if some risk factors for diabetes in adults over 50 are not modifiable:

- **Healthy Lifestyle:** A balanced diet and regular physical activity can greatly lower the chance of acquiring diabetes.

- **Weight management:** There is a reduced risk of diabetes if excess weight or healthy body weight are decreased. Blood sugar regulation can benefit from even small weight loss.

- **Routine Checkups:** Routine health examinations, which should include blood sugar testing, are crucial, particularly for people who have a family history of diabetes or other risk factors.

- **Education and Awareness:** People may make wise lifestyle decisions and seek the proper medical care by being more knowledgeable about diabetes and its risk factors.

In conclusion, diabetes management necessitates a diverse strategy because it is a common health risk among persons over 50. However, people and healthcare professionals can collaborate to manage the illness efficiently and enhance the quality of life for older persons with diabetes by being aware of the risk factors, complications, and preventive measures related to diabetes in this age range.

What Is Glycemic Index?

The GI (Glycemic Index) is a measure of the effect of carbohydrate foods on blood sugar levels. It is particularly relevant for individuals with diabetes, as managing blood sugar levels is crucial to diabetes care. In this discussion, we will explore the concept of glycemic index, its implications for diabetes management, and various factors to consider when planning a healthy diet for individuals with diabetes.

Understanding Glycemic Index

For foods on a scale of 0 to 100, the glycemic index is broken down according to how fast their blood glucose levels are rising compared to pure glucose which has a GI of 100. Rapidly digested and absorbed foods with high levels of GI (70 or higher are responsible for a sharp increase in blood sugar. On the other hand, food with a lower GI (55 or below is taken up and absorbed more slowly leading to gradual and reduced increases in blood glucose. Between these two extremes are foods with a moderate gastrointestinal content.

Implications for Diabetes Management

Managing your blood glucose levels is essential to avoid complications in people with diabetes. By selecting foods with a lower glycemic index, it is possible to achieve more stable blood glucose control. High GI foods can cause spikes in blood sugar levels, requiring more insulin or medication to regulate them. On the other hand, low GI foods can help maintain more consistent blood sugar levels and may reduce the risk of developing long-term complications associated with diabetes.

Glycemic Index of Certain Foods

Low GI foods (0 to 55):

- Apples, Grapefruit, Oranges, And Many Other Fruits
- Barley, Bulgar,
- Non-Starchy Vegetables, Carrots, Greens
- Dairy: Plain Yogurt, Plain Greek Yogurt, Milk.
- Fruits: Pears, Apples, Berries (Such as Blueberries, Strawberries, Raspberries), Cherries, Peaches, Grapefruit, Plums, Oranges.
- High-Fiber Bran Cereal
- Legumes: Chickpeas, Lentils, Black Beans, Pinto Beans, Kidney Beans, Soybeans.
- Milk And Yogurt
- Legumes, Most Nuts, And Beans
- Non-starchy vegetables: Broccoli, kale, spinach, cauliflower, zucchini, asparagus, Brussels sprouts, bell peppers, eggplant.
- Nuts and seeds: Almonds, flaxseeds, cashews, walnuts, chia seeds, pumpkin seeds.
- Oatmeal, steel-cut or rolled
- Other foods: Olive oil, eggs, avocados, tofu.
- Pasta, parboiled (converted) rice.

- Quinoa
- Sweeteners: Stevia, erythritol.
- Whole grains: Quinoa, oats, barley, buckwheat, whole wheat, bulgur, rye.

Moderate GI foods (56 to 69):
- Brown rice
- Couscous
- Pita bread, rye bread
- Raisins

High GI foods (70 +):

- Honey and Sugar
- White bread and bagels
- Most snack foods
- White rice
- Most processed cereals and instant oatmeal, including bran flakes
- Potatoes
- Watermelon and pineapple

It's important to note that the glycemic index of foods can vary depending on several factors, including ripeness, preparation methods, and cooking techniques. Additionally, the GI values mentioned here are approximate and can vary slightly between different sources.

Factors Affecting Glycemic Index

The glycemic index of a food can be influenced by various factors:

- Carbohydrate type: Different types of carbohydrates, such as sugars, starches, and fibers, have varying effects on blood glucose levels. Simple sugars typically have higher GI values compared to complex carbohydrates and fiber-rich foods.
- Cooking and processing: The degree of cooking and processing can affect the GI of foods. Generally, overcooking or processing can increase the glycemic index.
- Ripeness: The ripeness of fruits can impact their glycemic index. Riper fruits tend to have a higher GI due to increased sugar content.
- Fat and fiber content: The presence of fats and dietary fiber in a meal can slow down digestion and absorption, resulting in a lower glycemic index.

Limitations of Glycemic Index
While the glycemic index provides valuable information, it has some limitations:
- Individual responses: GI values are determined based on average responses in a group of people. Individuals, however, are capable of changing their reaction to the same food due to differences in metabolism, gut health and other factors.
- Food combinations: Various factors, including the presence of fat, protein and other ingredients, can affect the glycemic index of a meal. The overall response may be reduced through the combination of high glucose products with low GI foods or by including proteins and healthy fats.
- Portion sizes: Glycemic index values are typically based on standardized portion sizes, which may not reflect real-world eating habits. The total amount of carbohydrates consumed also affects blood sugar levels, so portion control remains important.

Glycemic Index and Diabetes Diet
Incorporating low-GI foods into a balanced diabetes diet can provide several benefits:
- Better blood sugar control: Low GI foods help prevent rapid spikes and drops in blood sugar levels, promoting more stable glycemic control.
- Increased satiety: Low GI foods tend to be more filling and can help with appetite control and weight management.
- Heart health: Low GI foods are often associated with a healthier overall dietary pattern, including a higher fiber intake, whole grains, fruits, and vegetables, which can contribute to better cardiovascular health.

The assessment of the food glycemic index should be considered as part of diabetes management but it is equally essential to take a general approach to healthy eating.

Blood Sugar Levels in Diabetes
Diabetes is characterized by an aberrant metabolism of carbohydrates, resulting in increased blood sugar levels, also known as hyperglycemia (American Diabetes Association, 2021). Normally, insulin, a hormone produced by the pancreas, facilitates the uptake of glucose (a type of sugar) into cells, where it's used as an energy source. In diabetes, either the body's production of insulin is insufficient or its cells fail to respond properly to insulin, leading to high blood sugar levels (Evert et al., 2013).

A balanced diet is crucial for maintaining optimal blood sugar levels. Nutrient-dense, low-glycemic foods, which do not trigger a rapid rise in blood sugar levels, should be prioritized (Evert et al., 2013). Regular monitoring of blood sugar levels is also essential to assess the efficacy of dietary and lifestyle changes.

Various Tests for Blood Sugar Levels

There are several tests that provide insight into an individual's blood glucose levels:

Fasting Blood Sugar Test

A fasting blood sugar test measures glucose levels after an overnight fast. It's typically used for diagnosing prediabetes and diabetes. A level below 100 milligrams per deciliter (mg/dL) is considered normal, while 100 to 125 mg/dL indicates prediabetes, and 126 mg/dL or higher on two separate tests indicates diabetes (American Diabetes Association, 2021).

Oral Glucose Tolerance Test

An oral glucose tolerance test involves drinking a glucose-rich beverage after fasting and having blood glucose levels measured at intervals over the next two hours. This test is particularly useful in diagnosing gestational diabetes, a form of diabetes that can occur during pregnancy (Mayo Clinic, 2018).

Random Blood Sugar Test

In a random blood sugar test, blood is drawn at any time, irrespective of the last meal. If levels are 200 mg/dL or higher, it suggests diabetes (Mayo Clinic, 2018).

Hemoglobin A1C Test

The A1C test provides an average of blood sugar levels over the past two to three months. It's often used for diagnosing and monitoring diabetes (Mayo Clinic, 2018).

Managing blood sugar levels is crucial in diabetes. Regular testing and a well-rounded diet tailored to an individual's needs can help achieve this balance and reduce the risk of complications.

Chapter 1

Treat Diabetes with Diet and Exercise

It can be challenging to find a diabetic diet plan that you enjoy. Finding a diet plan that you are capable of following can be even harder! You've undoubtedly already been informed that food and exercise are crucial components of controlling type 2 diabetes if you or someone you know has it. It's not always easy to follow that counsel, even when your life depends on it. Here, I've done some of the legwork for you by providing a feast of suggestions, ideas, and guidance to support you as you stick to your diabetes food plan and exercise routine.

What Is the Most Effective Diabetic Diet Plan?

The alarming rate at which this condition has spread for a variety of causes is the primary reason for the popularity and acceptability of the diabetic diet.

The term "silent killer" generally refers to diabetes. It is unquestionably a pleasant sickness that is spreading quickly. But, contrary to popular assumption, age is not a factor. Until a few decades ago, it was believed that adults over 40 were the only ones affected by this delightful sickness. However, the data on people with diabetes imply a quite different picture.

The young generation is no longer immune to this disease due to a sedentary lifestyle and junk food culture. In 1985, diabetes was thought to impact 30 million people. By 2000, it had risen to a staggering 171 million. By 2030, the WHO predicts that the number will reach 366 million.

The greatest and simplest strategy to combat this silent killer is through a diabetic diet.

Any diabetic diet's primary goal is to help the patient maintain healthy body weight while also maintaining a normal blood sugar level. It mainly depends on the patient's age, sexual orientation, level of physical activity, and type of diabetes.

As the primary element of food that triggers the release of glucose or sugar in the blood, carbohydrates are strictly regulated in diabetic diets. Although carbohydrates cannot and should not be fully removed from food, the goal of this kind of diet is to limit their consumption to the bare minimum. No diet is fully acceptable for everyone because everyone has varied nutritional needs and health circumstances.

What foods make up the ideal diabetic diet?

No diet will be suitable for everyone, as was already mentioned. However, if you want to live without worrying about your diabetes, some rules must be followed.

- Opt for 4-5 small meals a day instead of 3 heavy meals
- Make it a point to include fresh fruits and vegetables in your daily meals.
- Every day, 1.4 ounces of fiber must be ingested.
- Whole grain foods should be substituted for fast and junk meals.
- Products should not include more than one added sugar and bakery item.
- Watch out for eating carbs two hours before going to bed.

As an alternative, you might choose one of the carefully designed diabetic diets that will meet all of your nutritional requirements. It's not necessary to worry about calorie counts or how many carbohydrates you eat.

Diabetic Meal Schedule

Physicians and registered dieticians advise diabetics to monitor or restrict their diet. In diabetes treatment, it is important to eat a healthy diet and live according to the way of life. The right guidance from a certified dietician makes it simpler to follow a diabetic diet meal plan.

You might plan your daily meals or mix and match them using this diet plan. This is done without compromising the amount of carbohydrates you need to consume.

Everybody has a different diabetic diet. For people with type 1 and type 2 diabetes, there is a separate meal plan. Type 1 diabetics need to be aware of what they eat and supplement it with insulin daily. On the other side, those who have type 2 diabetes need to lose weight.

A proper diabetic food plan for your particular kind of diabetes is provided below.

Meal plan for type 1 diabetics on a diabetic diet:
A person with this kind of diabetes must consume the proper amount of protein and carbohydrates. Due to the numerous difficulties associated with diabetes, creating a diet meal plan is crucial for this person.

Type 1 diabetics frequently develop complications such as heart disease, renal failure, and high blood pressure. For this reason, they should focus on food low in sodium, sugar, fat and cholesterol. In addition, meal plans for people with type 1 diabetes typically include a variety of high-fiber meals, such as fruits and green leafy vegetables. All this is done to lower blood pressure and stabilize the person's blood sugar level.

Meal plan for diabetics with type 2 diabetes:

Anyone with type 2 diabetes needs to keep an eye on their weight. A fiber-rich meal, such as fish with a high level of omega 3 fatty acids, healthy fats and carbohydrates, should be part of the diet plan in people with type 2 diabetes. For the most part, people with type 2 diabetes should avoid foods that are rich in fat, sodium, and cholesterol.

It is recommended to eat regularly and in small quantities for people with type 2 diabetes. If eaten in tiny pieces instead of a full meal, it is considerably simpler to control glucose levels.

For the whole day, sample diabetic meal plan:

Breakfast diet menu:
- ¾ C. blackberries
- 1 C. yogurt
- 2 4½-in waffles
- A C. of Coffee or tea

Lunch diet menu:
- ½ cup of cauliflower or ½ cup of broccoli
- 1 cup beans
- 12 crackers
- A diet soda

Dinner Diet menu:
- 1 cup of celery sticks
- In one hamburger bun, 4oz of hamburger. There's a total of 1 Tablespoon ketchup, 2 tomato slices and 2 lettuce leaves in it.
- Skim milk

It's true that eating a healthy diet will help to reduce the effects of diabetes.

General Diet Guide: Foods Permitted and Foods to Avoid

A person with diabetes does not necessarily need to follow an intensive food regimen. However, the majority of diabetic cooking tips emphasize making informed decisions and having a well-thought-out strategy. The real secret to controlling diabetes involves altering the sorts of foods that diabetics consume as well as their eating habits, which frequently involve portion management and scheduled mealtimes.

A diabetic doesn't actually need to adhere to a rigid diet. Instead, the best course of action for a diabetic is generally to establish a diet high in essential nutrients, low in calories, and low in fat. In addition to food choices, any diabetic needs also take into account eating on a regular schedule and portioning meals to keep near to the recommended serving size.

The idea of counting carbohydrates is one way to make dietary changes, which can be advantageous for those who use insulin. Despite the fact that tracking fats and proteins is not as important as tracking carbs, people with diabetes should nonetheless pay close attention to both of these nutrients.

Consumption of Sweets

The end of sweets is inevitable if you have diabetes. Even while the vast majority of diabetics try to stay away from sweets as much as possible, the vast majority of medical professionals believe that indulging in a treat once in a while is not going to cause any harm. The primary concern in this regard is ensuring that sweets are consumed in measured quantities and that they do not throw off the overall carbohydrate count for all meals consumed in a given day. It would appear that there is still room in the life of a diabetic for a little bit of sweetness.

Permitted Foods

Make the most of your calories by eating healthy foods. Pick wholesome carbohydrates, foods high in fiber, seafood, and "good" fats.

1. Healthy Carb: Glucose is produced by the breakdown of sugars and carbohydrates in the digestive process. Both sugars and starches can be classified as either simple or complex carbohydrates, depending on their level of complexity. Concentrate on good sources of carbohydrates, such as:

   - Fruits.
   - Vegetables.
   - Complete grains.
   - Leguminous plants, like beans and peas.

- Dairy goods with low-fat content, like milk and cheese.
- Avoid foods and beverages with extra fats, sweets, or sodium and less healthful carbs.

2. **Foods high in fiber:** All plant food components that your body cannot digest or absorb are considered to be dietary fiber. Fiber helps manage blood sugar levels and moderates how your body digests food. Fiber-rich foods include:

- Vegetables.
- Fruits.
- Nuts.
- Leguminous plants, like beans and peas.
- Complete grains.
- Fish is heart-healthy
- Eat seafood that is good for your heart at least twice every week. Fish high in omega-3 fatty acids include salmon, mackerel, tuna, and sardines. These omega-3s could guard against heart disease.
- Steer clear of fried fish and fish like cod that contain a lot of mercury.

3. Healthy fats: It can help to reduce your cholesterol levels by eating foods rich in phytosterols or monounsaturated fatty acids. Among them are:
   - Avocados.
   - Nuts.
   - Olive, Peanut, and canola oils.

Don't go overboard, though, as fats all contain a lot of calories.

Foods To Avoid

Diabetes accelerates the process through which your arteries get blocked and hardened, increasing your risk of heart disease and stroke. In addition, the following ingredients can be detrimental to your efforts to maintain a heart-healthy diet.

- **The saturated fats.** Steer clear of dairy goods with high-fat content and animal proteins like butter, beef, hot dogs, sausage, and bacon. Also, keep palm kernel and coconut oils to a minimum.
- **Trans fats.** Avoid trans fats, which are found in stick margarines, shortening, baked goods, and processed snack foods.
- **Sodium.** Your sodium consumption should be reduced to 2,300 mg per day. Your doctor may

advise you to decrease your goals if you have a higher blood pressure.

- **Cholesterol.** High-fat dairy products, high-fat animal proteins, egg yolks, liver, and other organ meats are all sources of cholesterol. Take a daily intake of no more than 200 mg cholesterol.

Making a Diet Plan

You can design a healthy diet using various strategies to help you maintain blood sugar levels that are within the normal range. You might discover that one or a combination of the following strategy works for you with the assistance of a dietitian:

My Plate Approach

The United States Department of Agriculture (USDA) has the MyPlate nutrition guide, which displaced the USDA's pyramid guide on June 2, 2011. Essentially, it is a plate plan specifying that a meal must consist of 30% grains, 40% vegetables, 10% fruits, and 20% protein. There is also a small quantity of dairy (product), such as a cup of yogurt or a glass of milk.

The Harvard School of Public Health updated this strategy in their Harvard Healthy Eating Plate. In their updated version, they have increased the proportion of veggies to fruits while maintaining the same proportion of whole grains and lean protein on the plate.

However, the American Diabetes Association advises making your own plate by following these straightforward steps;

"Draw a line through the center of your dinner plate. Then, cut it again on one side so that your platter has three portions.

1. Stuff the biggest compartment with non-starchy vegetables like:

    - Bok choy, spinach, carrots, lettuce, greens, and cabbage
    - tomatoes, broccoli, cauliflower, and green beans
    - vegetable juice, salsa, okra, beets, onion, and cucumber
    - turnips, peppers, and mushrooms

2. Next, arrange grains and starchy foods: in one of the smaller compartments.

    - Whole grains include bread such as rye, cream of wheat; pastas, rice, tortillas and dal or whole wheat and high fiber cereals; baked cereal like oatmeal grits, tortillas, corn starch.
    - Potatoes, sweet potatoes, corn, green peas, lima beans, winter squash; pretzels, low-fat

crackers, light popcorn and snack chips; stewed beans and peas such as pinto beans or black-eyed peas

3. Now you will place the protein into a second small area, for example:

- Lean cuts of pig and beef, like pork loin or sirloin; poultry without the skin, such as turkey or chicken; fish, such as salmon, tuna, cod, or catfish; and other seafood, such as shrimp, crab, clams, oysters, or mussels.
- Low-fat cheese, tofu, and eggs.

If your meal plan permits it, you can include either a serving of fruit or a serving of dairy products.

Pick moderate amounts of healthy fats. Use oils for cooking. Nuts, seeds, avocado, and vinaigrette are some healthful salad additions.

Add a low-calorie beverage, such as water, unsweetened tea, or coffee, to finish your meal.

It has been suggested that the amount of time before a meal that a diabetic should inject insulin will vary on the type of insulin they are using and whether the insulin has a long, medium, or short action time.

For instance, it is advised that the patient consume some long-acting carbohydrates before going to bed to prevent nighttime hypoglycemia (abnormally low blood sugar levels). This is the case when the patient has a low blood glucose measurement immediately before bedtime that is below 6 millimoles per liter (108 mg/dL).

The recommendation for people with diabetes who use insulin or other medications like sulphonylureas is to avoid consuming alcohol on an empty stomach. This is one of the don'ts when it comes to alcohol. This is because alcohol prevents the liver's ability to make glycogen, which is a polysaccharide used to store glucose, and because some medications reduce the need to eat. Hypoglycemia can result from this in addition to the memory, judgment, and focus problems some medicines can induce.

Carbohydrate Tally

Carbohydrates have the biggest impact on your blood sugar level since they convert to sugar when consumed. Therefore, you might need to learn how to calculate the amount of carbohydrates you are eating with the aid of a nutritionist in order to assist in controlling your blood sugar. The insulin dosage can then be changed accordingly. It is thus essential to monitor the content of carbohydrates in each meal and snack.

You can learn portion control techniques from a dietitian, who can also help you become a knowledgeable label reader. Additionally, you can discover how to pay close attention to portion size and carbohydrate content.

Glycemic Index

This has been explained in great detail above.

The following are a few well-known diabetes-friendly diets:

Pritikin Diet

Nearly all of the items consumed on the Pritikin Diet are naturally grown and processed, including fruits, vegetables, cereals, lean meats, and seafood.

Low-Carb Diet

Popularized by the Atkins Diet, low-carb diets severely restrict the amount of carbohydrates and refined sugar consumed.

High-Fiber Diet

A high-fiber diet, which only includes foods that are high in fiber, has been proven to have the same blood sugar-lowering effects as oral diabetes medications.

Vegan Diet

Solely fruits, vegetables, and other cultivated foods.

Exercise in Diabetes Management

A fundamental element of the management of diabetes is to regularly exercise. Whether an individual has type 1 or type 2 diabetes, incorporating physical activity into their daily routine offers numerous benefits in managing blood glucose levels, improving overall health, and reducing the risk of complications associated with diabetes. This segment explores the importance of exercise in diabetes management, outlining the specific advantages and considerations for individuals with diabetes.

Blood Glucose Control

Exercise has a profound impact on blood glucose control. During physical activity, muscles require energy, which is primarily derived from glucose. As a result, exercising helps lower blood glucose levels by increasing glucose uptake into the muscles without the need for insulin. In addition, exercise has an effect on insulin sensitivity and allows more efficient use of insulin by the body. This effect persists even after the exercise session, leading to improved glucose control throughout the day.

Weight Management

Being overweight or obese is a major risk factor for the development of type 2 diabetes and can make the condition worse in people who already have diabetes. Regular exercise plays a vital role in weight management and can help individuals achieve and maintain healthy body weight. Physical activity helps burn calories, build lean muscle mass, and increase metabolism, which aids in weight loss or weight maintenance. Individuals with diabetes may be more able to manage blood glucose levels and decrease insulin resistance if they maintain their normal weight.

Cardiovascular Health

Diabetes is strongly associated with an increased risk of cardiovascular diseases such as heart attacks and strokes. An exercise is a powerful tool for improving cardiovascular health, reducing the risk of these complications, and managing other cardiovascular risk factors such as high blood pressure and unhealthy cholesterol levels. Regular physical activity strengthens the heart, improves blood circulation, lowers blood pressure, and enhances lipid profiles, leading to a healthier cardiovascular system.

Insulin Sensitivity and Medication Management

Regular exercise enhances insulin sensitivity, meaning the body can use insulin more effectively to transport glucose into the cells. As a result, individuals with diabetes may require lower doses of medication, particularly for type 2 diabetes. Exercise should be incorporated alongside proper medical guidance, as medication adjustments may be necessary to prevent hypoglycemia (low blood sugar) during and after physical activity.

Stress Management and Mental Health

Diabetes management can often be accompanied by stress and emotional challenges. Exercise has proven benefits in reducing stress, anxiety, and depression, all of which can affect blood glucose control. Physical exercise stimulates the release of neurotransmitters like endorphins and natural feelgood hormones in the body, giving rise to a positive mood and overall mental health. Engaging in regular exercise can serve as an effective coping mechanism, enhancing the individual's ability to manage the emotional aspects of living with diabetes.

Long-Term Complication Prevention

Exercise plays a significant role in reducing the risk of long-term complications associated with diabetes. By managing blood glucose levels, weight, and cardiovascular health, exercise helps prevent complications such as diabetic neuropathy (nerve damage), retinopathy (eye damage), nephropathy (kidney damage), and peripheral vascular disease. Regular physical activity, combined with other essential aspects of diabetes management, can significantly improve long-term outcomes and quality of life for individuals with diabetes.

On the whole, it should be noted that it is important for individuals with diabetes to consult with their healthcare team before initiating or modifying an exercise regimen, as personalized guidance is essential to ensure safety and optimize the benefits of exercise in diabetes management.

Types of Exercise
- **Aerobic exercise:** Understanding the benefits of aerobic activities like walking, jogging, swimming, and cycling.
- **Strength training:** The necessity of building muscle mass and integrating resistance training.
- **Flexibility and balance exercises:** The role of stretching, yoga, and tai chi in maintaining flexibility, balance, and preventing injuries.

Exercise Guidelines for Diabetes
- **Frequency and duration:** Recommended frequency and duration of exercise sessions for optimal diabetes management.
- **Precautions and safety:** Pre-exercise evaluations, blood sugar monitoring, and safety considerations for individuals with diabetes.
- **Modification of exercises for complications:** changes in exercise regimens when associated with the presence of diabetes related complications.
- **Incorporating physical activity into daily life:** Strategies for increasing daily physical activity, such as taking the stairs or walking breaks.

Chapter 2:

4-Week Meal Plan

Here is a 4 weeks meal plan for a diabetic person who is 50 years old. Please note that this is only a general plan, so it's crucial that you speak with a registered dietitian or other healthcare experts to customize your meal plans based on your unique requirements, preferences, and any other medical issues you might be experiencing.

Week 1

Days	Breakfast	A.m/P.m Snack	Lunch	Dinner
Monday	Veggie Omelet	Greek Yogurt with Berries	Baked Lemon Herb Salmon	Grilled Lemon Herb Chicken
Tuesday	Greek Yogurt Parfait	Veggie Sticks with Hummus	Grilled Shrimp Skewers	Herb-Roasted Chicken Breast with Vegetables
Wendesday	Whole Grain Pancakes	Baked Sweet Potato Fries	Lemon Garlic Baked Salmon	Grilled Teriyaki Chicken Stir-Fry
Thursday	Avocado Toast with Poached Egg	Caprese Skewers	Tuna Salad Lettuce Wraps	Grilled Herb-Marinated Turkey Tenderloin
Friday	Spinach and Mushroom Breakfast Wrap	Baked Kale Chips	Baked White Fish with Tomatoes and Olives	Oven-Roasted Turkey Breast
Saturday	Veggie Omelet	Quick Lemon-Blueberry Bites	Grilled Salmon with Avocado Salsa	Grilled Balsamic Glazed Pork Chops
Sunday	Greek Yogurt Parfait	Cottage Cheese and Tomato Salad	Garlic and Herb Baked Shrimp	Chicken and Broccoli Stir-Fry

Week 2

Days	Breakfast	A.m/P.m Snack	Lunch	Dinner
Monday	Spinach and Mushroom Breakfast Wrap	Guacamole with Veggie Slices	Baked Lemon Dijon Tilapia	Herb-Roasted Chicken Breast with Vegetables
Tuesday	Veggie Omelet	Baked Zucchini Chips	Grilled Lemon Garlic Halibut	Grilled Herb-Marinated Turkey Tenderloin
Wendesday	Greek Yogurt Parfait	Deviled Eggs	Baked Dijon Salmon	Chicken and Broccoli Stir-Fry
Thursday	Whole Grain Pancakes	Apple Slices with Peanut Butter	Thai Coconut Curry Shrimp	Oven-Roasted Turkey Breast
Friday	Avocado Toast with Poached Egg	Roasted Chickpeas	Lemon Pepper Grilled Tuna Steaks	Grilled Balsamic Glazed Pork Chops
Saturday	Greek Yogurt Parfait	Cucumber and Smoked Salmon Roll-Ups	Pesto Shrimp with Zucchini Noodles	Grilled Lemon Herb Chicken
Sunday	Veggie Omelet	Baked Parmesan Zucchini Fries	Baked Parmesan Crusted Haddock	Grilled Teriyaki Chicken Stir-Fry

The Diabetic Cookbook After 50

Week 3

Days	Breakfast	A.m/P.m Snack	Lunch	Dinner
Monday	Spinach and Mushroom Breakfast Wrap	Turkey Lettuce Wraps	Shrimp and Avocado Salad	Herb-Crusted Baked Chicken Thighs
Tuesday	Veggie Omelet	Baked Eggplant Chips	Mixed Greens Salad with Grilled Chicken	Turkey Meatballs with Zucchini Noodles
Wendesday	Greek Yogurt Parfait	Spicy Roasted Edamame	Lentil Soup	Grilled Herb-Marinated Turkey Tenderloin
Thursday	Whole Grain Pancakes	Baked Buffalo Cauliflower Bites	Spinach and Berry Salad	Grilled Balsamic Glazed Pork Chops
Friday	Avocado Toast with Poached Egg	Mini Bell Pepper Nachos	Tomato Basil Soup	Chicken and Broccoli Stir-Fry
Saturday	Greek Yogurt Parfait	Roasted Honeynut Squash	Quinoa and Vegetable Salad	Oven-Roasted Turkey Breast
Sunday	Veggie Omelet	Greek Yogurt with Berries	Chicken Vegetable Soup	Grilled Lemon Herb Chicken

Week 4

Days	Breakfast	A.m/P.m Snack	Lunch	Dinner
Monday	Spinach and Mushroom Breakfast Wrap	Veggie Sticks with Hummus	Greek Salad	Turkey Meatballs with Zucchini Noodles
Tuesday	Veggie Omelet	Baked Sweet Potato Fries	Minestrone Soup	Grilled Herb-Marinated Turkey Tenderloin
Wendesday	Greek Yogurt Parfait	Caprese Skewers	Tuna Salad with Avocado	Chicken and Broccoli Stir-Fry
Thursday	Whole Grain Pancakes	Baked Kale Chips	Butternut Squash Soup	Oven-Roasted Turkey Breast
Friday	Avocado Toast with Poached Egg	Quick Lemon-Blueberry Bites	Roasted Beet and Orange Salad	Grilled Balsamic Glazed Pork Chops
Saturday	Greek Yogurt Parfait	Cottage Cheese and Tomato Salad	Chicken Tortilla Soup	Grilled Lemon Herb Chicken
Sunday	Veggie Omelet	Guacamole with Veggie Slices	Spinach and Feta Soup	Grilled Teriyaki Chicken Stir-Fry

Chapter 3:

Breakfast Recipes

Avocado Toast with Poached Egg

Cooking Time: 5 mins   **Preparation Time:** 10 mins   **Servings:** 2

Ingredients:

- 2 slices whole grain bread
- 1 ripe avocado
- 2 large eggs
- 1 tablespoon lemon juice
- Pepper and salt to taste
- Fresh parsley for garnish (optional)

Instructions:

1. Toast the slices of whole grain bread until golden brown.
2. In a bowl, with lemon juice, salt, and pepper mash the ripe avocado.
3. Distribute the mashed avocado evenly over the toast.
4. Add a splash of vinegar to a saucepan of water and bring to a simmer.
5. Carefully break eggs into boiling water and poach for 3-4 minutes, till white is set but yolk is still runny.
6. Carefully spoon the poached eggs out of the water and lay on top of the avocado toast.
7. If you like, top with fresh parsley.
8. Serve immediately.

Nutrition Facts:

Per serving: Calories: 320 kcal, Carbs: 26 g, Proteins: 12 g, Fats: 18 g

Greek Yogurt Parfait

Cooking Time: 5 mins   **Preparation Time:** 0 mins   **Servings:** 2

Ingredients:

- 1 cup plain Greek yogurt (low-fat)
- 1/4 cup fresh blueberries
- 1/4 cup fresh strawberries (sliced)
- 2 tablespoons chopped almonds
- 1 tablespoon honey (optional)

Instructions:

1. In a glass or a bowl, layer the Greek yogurt, blueberries, and strawberries.
2. Sprinkle chopped almonds on top.
3. Drizzle honey over the parfait for added sweetness if desired.
4. Serve immediately.

Nutrition Facts:

Per serving: Calories: 200 kcal, Carbs: 17g, Proteins: 20 g, Fats: 6 g

The Diabetic Cookbook After 50

Spinach and Mushroom Breakfast Wrap

⏲ *Cooking Time: 10 mins* 🍳 *Preparation Time: 10 mins* 🔔 *Servings: 2*

Ingredients:

- *2 whole grain tortillas*
- *1 cup fresh spinach leaves*
- *1/2 cup sliced mushrooms*
- *2 large eggs*
- *2 tablespoons low-fat shredded cheese*
- *1 tablespoon olive oil*
- *Pepper and salt to taste*

Instructions:

1. Heat olive oil in a skillet over medium heat.
2. Add mushrooms and sauté till they soften.
3. Add spinach to the pan and cook till wilted.
4. In a separate bowl, whisk the eggs and season Pour the whisked eggs into the skillet and scramble until cooked through.
5. Warm the tortillas in a microwave or on a stovetop.
6. Divide the scrambled eggs, spinach, and mushrooms evenly between the tortillas.
7. Sprinkle shredded cheese on top.
8. Roll up the tortillas to form wraps.
9. Serve warm.

Nutrition Facts:
Per serving: Calories: 290 kcal, Carbs: 23 g, Proteins: 15 g, Fats: 14g

Veggie Omelet

⏲ *Cooking Time: 10 mins* 🍳 *Preparation Time: 10 mins* 🔔 *Servings: 2*

Ingredients:

- *4 large eggs*
- *1/4 cup diced bell peppers*
- *1/4 cup diced onions*
- *1/4 cup diced tomatoes*
- *1/4 cup chopped spinach*
- *1/4 cup shredded low-fat cheese*
- *1 tablespoon olive oil*
- *Pepper and salt to taste*

Instructions:

1. Heat olive oil in a non-stick pan on a moderate heat.
2. Add onions and bell peppers to the skillet and sauté until they soften.
3. In a bowl, whisk the eggs and season using pepper and salt.
4. Pour the whisked eggs into the skillet and cook for almost a minute.
5. Sprinkle tomatoes, spinach, and shredded cheese evenly over the omelet.
6. Fold the omelet in half and cook for further 2-3 minutes till the cheese melts.
7. Serve hot.

Nutrition Facts:
Per serving: Calories: 220 kcal, Carbs: 7 g, Proteins: 16 g, Fats: 15 g

Whole Grain Pancakes

Cooking Time: 10 mins   *Preparation Time: 10 mins*   *Servings: 2*

Ingredients:

- *1 cup whole wheat flour*
- *1 teaspoon baking powder*
- *1/2 teaspoon cinnamon*
- *1/4 teaspoon salt*
- *1 cup low-fat milk*
- *1 large egg*
- *1 tablespoon canola oil*
- *1 tablespoon honey (optional)*
- *Fresh berries for topping (optional)*

Instructions:

1. In a mixing bowl, whisk together the baking powder, whole wheat flour, salt and cinnamon.
2. In a different bowl, blend the milk, egg, canola oil, and honey (optional).
3. To mix the wet and the dry stuffs, stir them until they are mixed well.
4. Heat a griddle or nonstick skillet to medium and lightly coat with cooking spray.
5. Until bubbles form on the surface, then flip and cook for an additional three minutes till golden brown.
6. Serve the pancakes with a sprinkling of fresh berries on top, if you like.

Nutrition Facts:

Per serving: Calories: 220 kcal, Carbs: 34 g, Proteins: 8 g, Fats: 6 g

Chapter 4:

Snack and Side

Greek Yogurt with Berries

⏲ *Cooking Time: No* 📇 *Preparation Time: 5 mins* 🛎 *Servings: 2*

🛍 Ingredients:

- *1 cup plain Greek yogurt*
- *1/2 cup mixed berries (such as strawberries, blueberries, raspberries)*

🥣 Instructions:

1. Place the Greek yogurt in a bowl.
2. Wash the mixed berries and add them to the bowl.
3. Gently mix the yogurt and berries together.
4. Serve and enjoy!

Nutrition Facts:

Per serving: Calories: 150 kcal, Carbs: 15 g, Proteins: 15 g, Fats: 0g

Baked Sweet Potato Fries

⏲ *Cooking Time: 4-6 mins* 📇 *Preparation Time: 10 mins* 🛎 *Servings: 2*

🛍 Ingredients:

- *4 tuna steaks (4-6 ounces each)*
- *2 tablespoons olive oil*
- *2 tablespoons fresh lemon juice*
- *1 teaspoon lemon zest*
- *1 teaspoon freshly ground black pepper*
- *1/2 teaspoon salt*
- *1/2 teaspoon dried dill*
- *Lemon wedges for serving*
- *Fresh dill for garnish*

🥣 Instructions:

1. Preheat the oven to 425°F (220°C).
2. Cut the sweet potatoes into fry shapes.
3. In a large bowl, toss the sweet potato fries with olive oil, salt, and pepper.
4. Spread the fries evenly on a baking sheet lined with parchment paper.
5. Bake for about 20-25 mins, till the fries are crispy and golden.
6. Remove from the oven and let them cool slightly before serving.

Nutrition Facts:

Per serving: Calories: 120 kcal, Carbos: 25 g, Proteins: 2 g Fats: 3 g

Veggie Sticks with Hummus

Cooking Time: No   *Preparation Time: 5 mins*   *Servings: 2*

Ingredients:

- *Carrot sticks, cucumber slices, bell pepper strips*
- *2 tablespoons hummus*

Instructions:

1. Wash and cut carrot sticks, cucumber slices, and bell pepper strips.
2. Place the hummus in a small serving bowl.
3. Arrange the veggie sticks around the bowl of hummus.
4. Serve and dip the veggie sticks into the hummus.

Nutrition Facts:

Per serving: Calories: 80 kcal, Carbs: 10 g, Protein: 2 g, Fat: 4g

Caprese Skewers

Cooking Time: No   *Preparation Time: 15 mins*   *Servings: 2*

Ingredients:

- *Cherry tomatoes*
- *Fresh mozzarella balls*
- *Fresh basil leaves*

Instructions:

1. Wash the cherry tomatoes and basil leaves.
2. Skewer one mozzarella ball, one cherry tomato, and one basil leaf onto each skewer.
3. Arrange the skewers on a serving platter.
4. Serve.

Nutrition Facts:

Per serving: Calories: 100 kcal, Carbs: 3 g, Proteins: 6 g, Fats: 7 g

Baked Kale Chips

Cooking Time: 10-15mins *Preparation Time: 10 mins* *Servings: 2*

Ingredients:
- *1 bunch of fresh kale*
- *1 tablespoon olive oil*
- *1/2 teaspoon sea salt*
- *1/4 teaspoon garlic powder*

Nutrition Facts:

Per serving: Calories: 50 kcal, Fats: 3.5 g, Carbos: 5 g, Proteins: 2 g

Instructions:
1. Preheat the oven to 350°F (175°C).
2. Wash the kale leaves thoroughly and pat them dry.
3. Remove the tough stems from the kale leaves and tear them into bite-sized pieces.
4. Place the torn kale leaves in a large bowl and drizzle with olive oil. Toss well to ensure all the leaves are coated with oil.
5. Sprinkle sea salt and garlic powder over the kale leaves and toss again to evenly distribute the seasonings.
6. Arrange the kale leaves in a single layer on a baking sheet lined with parchment paper.
7. Bake in the preheated oven for about 10-15 minutes or until the edges of the leaves are crispy and lightly browned.
8. Remove from the oven and let the kale chips cool for a few minutes before serving.

Cottage Cheese and Tomato Salad

Cooking Time: 12-15 *Preparation Time: 15 mins* *Servings: 2*

Ingredients:
- *1 cup low-fat cottage cheese*
- *1 medium tomato, diced*
- *1 tablespoon chopped fresh basil*
- *Pepper and salt to taste*

Instructions:
1. In a bowl, combine the low-fat cottage cheese, diced tomato, chopped fresh basil, salt, and pepper.
2. Mix gently to combine.
3. Serve immediately or refrigerate until ready to serve.

Nutrition Facts:

Per serving: Calories: 150 Kcal, Carbos: 10 g, Proteins: 20 g, Fat: 3 g

Quick Lemon-Blueberry Bites

Cooking Time: 12-15mins *Preparation Time: 15 mins* *Servings: 2*

Ingredients:

- 2 tablespoons all-purpose flour
- 2 tablespoons whole-wheat pastry flour
- 1/8 teaspoon baking soda
- 1/8 teaspoon cream of tartar
- pinch of salt
- 1/4 cup granulated sugar
- 1 1/4 tablespoons unsalted butter, softened
- 1/4 of a large egg (lightly beaten, thendivided)
- 1/2 teaspoon finely grated lemon zest
- 1/2 teaspoon lemon juice
- 1/4 teaspoon lemon extract
- 1/4 cup fresh blueberries

Instructions:

1. Incorporate the up the whole-wheat pastry flour, all-purpose flour, cream of tartar, baking soda, and salt in a medium mixing basin.
2. In a mixing bowl, use an electric mixer on medium-high speed to beat the granulated sugar and softened butter until the mixture is light and fluffy.
3. Add half of the lightly beaten egg, along with the finely grated lemon zest, lemon juice, and lemon extract to the sugar and butter mixture. Beat until the ingredients are well blended.
4. Subsequently add the flour blend to the bowl, mixing on low speed just till incorporated. Chill the dough for almost 30 mins, covered.
5. Preheat the oven to 375°f and line a small baking sheet with parchment paper or a nonstick baking mat.
6. With moistened hands, roll the dough into 4 balls, using about 2 level teaspoons of dough for each ball. Lightly smooth the balls, then set them on the lined baking sheet, allowing some space among each.
7. Arrange 3 fresh blueberries on top of each cookie.
8. Bake the cookies in the preheated oven for 8 to 10 mins, till they appear puffed and have a light golden-brown color around the edges.
9. After the cookies have cooled on the baking tray for two minutes, move them to a wire rack to finish cooling.

Nutrition Facts:

Per serving: Calories: 190 kcal, Carbs: 28 g, Protein: 3g, Fat: 0g

Guacamole with Veggie Slices

Cooking Time: No *Preparation Time: 10 mins* *Servings: 2*

Ingredients:
- 1 ripe avocado
- 1 small tomato, diced
- 1 tablespoon lime juice
- Pepper and salt to taste
- Carrot sticks, cucumber slices, bell pepper strips for dipping

Instructions:
1. Cut the ripe avocado in half, remove the pit, and scoop out the flesh into a bowl.
2. Mash the avocado with a fork until smooth.
3. Add diced tomato, lime juice, salt, and pepper to the mashed avocado.
4. Mix well to combine.
5. Serve the guacamole with carrot sticks, cucumber slices, and bell pepper strips for dipping.

Nutrition Facts:
Per serving: Calories: 180 kcal, Carbs: 10 g, Protein: 3 g, Fats: 15 g

Baked Zucchini Chips

Cooking Time: 20-25 mins *Preparation Time: 15 mins* *Servings: 2*

Ingredients:
- 2 medium zucchini, sliced into thin rounds
- 1 tablespoon olive oil
- 1/4 teaspoon garlic powder
- Pepper and salt to taste

Instructions:
1. Preheat the oven to 425°F (220°C).
2. Slice the zucchini into thin rounds.
3. In a bowl, toss the zucchini slices with olive oil, garlic powder, salt, and pepper.
4. Arrange the slices on a baking sheet lined with parchment paper, making sure they're not overlapping.
5. Bake for about 15-20 minutes, flipping the slices halfway through, until they are golden and crispy.
6. Remove from the oven and let them cool slightly before serving.

Nutrition Facts:
Per serving: Calories: 80 kcal, Carbs: 6 g, Proteins: 2 g, Fats: 6 g

The Diabetic Cookbook After 50

Deviled Eggs

⏲ *Cooking Time: 10 mins* ⏱ *Preparation Time: 15 mins* 🔔 *Servings: 2*

Ingredients:
- *4 hard-boiled eggs, peeled*
- *2 tablespoons light mayonnaise*
- *1 teaspoon Dijon mustard*
- *Paprika (optional)*

Instructions:
1. Slice the hard-boiled eggs in half lengthwise.
2. Carefully remove the yolks and place them in a bowl.
3. Mash the yolks with a fork and mix in the light mayonnaise and Dijon mustard until smooth.
4. Spoon or pipe the yolk mixture back into the egg white halves.
5. Sprinkle with paprika, if desired.
6. Refrigerate until ready to serve.

Nutrition Facts:
Calories: 150 kcal Carbs: 2 g, Proteins: 12 g, Fats: 10g

Apple Slices with Peanut Butter

⏲ *Cooking Time: No* ⏱ *Preparation Time: 5 mins* 🔔 *Servings: 2*

Ingredients:
- *1 medium apple, sliced*
- *1 tablespoon natural peanut butter (without added sugar)*

Instructions:
1. Wash and slice the apple into thin rounds or wedges.
2. Spread the natural peanut butter on one side of each apple slice.
3. Press two slices together to create a peanut butter-filled apple slice.
4. Repeat with the remaining slices.
5. Serve.

Nutrition Facts:
Per serving: Calories: 160 kcal, Carbs: 20 g, Proteins: 4 g, Fats: 8 g

Roasted Chickpeas

⏲ *Cooking Time: 30-35 mins* 🍳 *Preparation Time: 10 mins* 🔔 *Servings: 2*

Ingredients:
- *1 can (15 ounces) chickpeas, drained and rinsed*
- *1 tablespoon olive oil*
- *1 teaspoon paprika*
- *1/2 teaspoon garlic powder*
- *Pepper and salt to taste*

Instructions:
1. Preheat the oven to 400°F (200°C).
2. Drain and rinse the chickpeas, then pat them dry with a towel.
3. In a bowl, toss the chickpeas with olive oil, paprika, garlic powder, salt, and pepper.
4. Spread the chickpeas evenly on a baking sheet lined with parchment paper.
5. Roast in the oven for about 25-30 minutes, shaking the pan occasionally, until the chickpeas are crispy and golden.
6. Remove from the oven and let them cool before serving.

Nutrition Facts:
Per serving: Calories: 140 kcal, Carbs: 22 g, Proteins: 6 g, Fats: 3g

Cucumber and Smoked Salmon Roll-Ups

⏲ *Cooking Time: No* 🍳 *Preparation Time: 5 mins* 🔔 *Servings: 2*

Ingredients:
- *2 large cucumbers*
- *4 ounces of smoked salmon*
- *4 tablespoons of cream cheese (low-fat or light version)*
- *1 tablespoon of fresh dill, chopped*
- *Pepper and salt to taste*

Nutrition Facts:
Per serving: Calories: 95 kcal, Carbs: 4 g, Proteins: 7 g Fats: 6 g

Instructions:
1. Wash the cucumbers and cut off the ends. Slice the cucumbers lengthwise into thin strips using a mandoline or vegetable peeler.
2. In a small bowl, combine the cream cheese, chopped dill, salt, and pepper. Mix well until the ingredients are evenly incorporated.
3. Lay the cucumber slices on a clean surface and pat them dry with a paper towel.
4. Spread a thin layer of the cream cheese mixture onto each cucumber slice.
5. Place a slice of smoked salmon on top of the cream cheese layer.
6. Roll up each cucumber slice tightly, securing it with a toothpick if needed.
7. Repeat the process until all the cucumber slices are used.
8. Serve the roll-ups immediately or refrigerate them for a refreshing snack later.

Baked Parmesan Zucchini Fries

⏱ **Cooking Time:** 25-30 mins 🍳 **Preparation Time:** 15 mins 🍽 **Servings:** 2

🛒 Ingredients:

- 2 medium zucchini
- 1/4 cup grated Parmesan cheese
- 1/4 cup almond flour
- 1 teaspoon garlic powder
- 1 teaspoon dried oregano
- Pepper and salt to taste
- Cooking spray

🍲 Instructions:

1. Preheat the oven to 425°F (220°C) and line a baking sheet with parchment paper.
2. Cut the zucchini into sticks similar in size to French fries.
3. In a shallow bowl, combine the grated Parmesan cheese, almond flour, garlic powder, dried oregano, salt, and pepper.
4. Dip each zucchini stick into the Parmesan mixture, coating it evenly, and place it on the prepared baking sheet.
5. Repeat the process with all the zucchini sticks.
6. Lightly spray the coated zucchini sticks with cooking spray to help them crisp up.
7. Bake in the preheated oven for about 20-25 minutes or until the zucchini fries are golden brown and crispy.
8. Remove from the oven and serve immediately.

Nutrition Facts:

Per serving: Calories: 80 kcal, Carbs: 5 g, Proteins: 5 g, Fats: 5 g

Turkey Lettuce Wraps

⏱ **Cooking Time:** No 🍳 **Preparation Time:** 15 mins 🍽 **Servings:** 2

🛒 Ingredients:

- 8 large lettuce leaves (such as iceberg or romaine)
- 8 ounces lean ground turkey
- 1/2 cup diced bell peppers (assorted colors)
- 1/2 cup diced tomatoes
- 1/4 cup diced red onions
- 1/4 cup shredded carrots
- 1 tablespoon low-sodium soy sauce
- 1 tablespoon olive oil
- 1 teaspoon minced garlic
- Pepper and salt to taste

🍲 Instructions:

1. In a large skillet, heat olive oil over medium heat. Add minced garlic and sauté until fragrant.
2. Add the ground turkey to the skillet and cook until browned, breaking it up into smaller pieces with a spatula.
3. Stir in the diced bell peppers, tomatoes, red onions, and shredded carrots. Cook for an additional 3-4 minutes or until the vegetables are slightly softened.
4. Pour in the low-sodium soy sauce and season with pepper and salt. Stir well to combine all the ingredients and cook for another minute.
5. Remove the skillet from heat and let the mixture cool slightly.
6. Assemble the lettuce wraps by spooning the turkey mixture onto each lettuce leaf.
7. Fold the sides of the lettuce over the filling and roll it up tightly.
8. Secure the wraps with toothpicks if necessary and serve.

Nutrition Facts:

Per serving: Calories: 120 kcal, Carbs: 7 g, Proteins: 13 g, Fats: 5 g

Baked Eggplant Chips

⌚ **Cooking Time:** 20mins   🍽 **Preparation Time:** 15 mins   🛎 **Servings:** 2

🛍 Ingredients:

- *1 medium eggplant*
- *2 tablespoons olive oil*
- *1 teaspoon garlic powder*
- *1/2 teaspoon paprika*
- *1/2 teaspoon dried basil*
- *Pepper and salt to taste*

🍳 Instructions:

1. Preheat the oven to 400°F (200°C) and line a baking sheet with parchment paper.
2. Wash the eggplant and slice it into thin rounds, about 1/4 inch thick.
3. In a small bowl, combine the olive oil, garlic powder, paprika, dried basil, salt, and pepper.
4. Place the eggplant slices on the prepared baking sheet and brush both sides with the olive oil mixture.
5. Bake in the preheated oven for about 15-20 minutes, flipping the slices halfway through until they are golden brown and crispy.
6. Remove from the oven and let the chips cool for a few minutes before serving.

Nutrition Facts:
Per serving: Calories: 70 kcal, Carbs: 8 g, Proteins: 1 g, Fats: 4 g

Spicy Roasted Edamame

⌚ **Cooking Time:** 15-20mins   🍽 **Preparation Time:** 10 mins   🛎 **Servings:** 2

🛍 Ingredients:

- *1 cup frozen edamame (shelled)*
- *1 tablespoon olive oil*
- *1/2 teaspoon chili powder*
- *1/4 teaspoon cayenne pepper*
- *1/4 teaspoon garlic powder*
- *1/4 teaspoon smoked paprika*
- *Salt to taste*

🍳 Instructions:

1. Preheat the oven to 400°F (200°C) and line a baking sheet with parchment paper.
2. In a bowl, combine the frozen edamame, olive oil, chili powder, cayenne pepper, garlic powder, smoked paprika, and salt. Toss well to coat the edamame evenly.
3. Spread the seasoned edamame in a single layer on the prepared baking sheet.
4. Bake in the preheated oven for about 15-20 minutes, stirring once or twice during cooking, until the edamame is crispy and slightly golden.
5. Remove from the oven and let the edamame cool before serving.

Nutrition Facts:
Per serving: Calories: 90 kcal, Carbs: 6 g, Proteins: 7 g, Fats: 4 g

Baked Buffalo Cauliflower Bites

⏲ **Cooking Time:** 25-30 mins 🍳 **Preparation Time:** 15 mins 🍽 **Servings:** 2

Ingredients:
- 1 medium head of cauliflower
- 1/4 cup almond flour
- 1/4 cup unsweetened almond milk
- 2 tablespoons hot sauce (check the label for low sugar and sodium content)
- 1 tablespoon olive oil
- 1 teaspoon garlic powder
- 1/2 teaspoon paprika
- Pepper and salt to taste

Nutrition Fact:

Per serving: Calories: 70 kcal, Carb: 8 g, Proteins: 3 g Fats: 4g

Instructions:
1. Preheat the oven to 450°F (230°C) and line a baking sheet with parchment paper.
2. Cut the cauliflower into bite-sized florets.
3. In a bowl, whisk together almond flour, almond milk, hot sauce, olive oil, garlic powder, paprika, salt, and pepper until well combined.
4. Add the cauliflower florets to the bowl and toss them in the mixture until evenly coated.
5. Place the coated cauliflower florets in a single layer on the prepared baking sheet.
6. Bake in the preheated oven for about 20-25 minutes, flipping the florets halfway through until they are crispy and lightly browned.
7. Remove from the oven and let the cauliflower bites cool for a few minutes before serving.

Mini Bell Pepper Nachos

⏲ **Cooking Time:** 10 mins 🍳 **Preparation Time:** 15 mins 🍽 **Servings:** 2

Ingredients:
- 8 mini bell peppers (assorted colors)
- 1/2 cup lean ground turkey or chicken
- 1/4 cup diced tomatoes
- 1/4 cup diced red onions
- 1/4 cup shredded reduced-fat cheddar cheese
- 1/4 cup sliced black olives
- 1 tablespoon olive oil
- 1 teaspoon chili powder
- 1/2 teaspoon cumin
- Pepper and salt to taste

Nutrition Facts:

Per serving: Calories: 80 kcal, Carb: 6 g, Proteins: 7 Fats: 4g

Instructions:
1. Preheat the oven to 400°F (200°C) and line a baking sheet with parchment paper.
2. Cut the mini bell peppers in half lengthwise and remove the seeds and membranes.
3. In a skillet, heat olive oil over medium heat. Add the ground turkey or chicken and cook until browned, breaking it up into smaller pieces with a spatula.
4. Stir in the diced tomatoes, red onions, chili powder, cumin, salt, and pepper. Cook for an additional 3-4 minutes or until the vegetables are slightly softened.
5. Place the bell pepper halves on the prepared baking sheet, and cut side up.
6. Spoon the turkey or chicken mixture into each bell pepper half.
7. Top each pepper with shredded cheddar cheese and sliced black olives.
8. Bake in the preheated oven for about 10-12 minutes or until the cheese is melted and bubbly.
9. Remove from the oven and let the mini bell pepper nachos cool for a few minutes before serving.

Roasted Honeynut Squash

Cooking Time: 30 mins *Preparation Time: 10 mins* *Servings: 2*

Ingredients:

- *1 medium honeynut squash, halved lengthwise and seeded*
- *2 teaspoons butter*
- *Pinch of salt, ground pepper and cinnamon*

Instructions:

1. Oven should be heated to 425°F.
2. Place the squash halves on a baking pan, cut side up. Fill each cavity with 1 tsp butter. Season using pepper, salt, and cinnamon to taste. Roast for 25 to 30 minutes, or till the vegetables are soft.

Nutrition Facts:

Per serving: Calories: 114 kcal, Carbs: 21 g, Proteins: 2 g, Fats: 4 g

Chapter 5:

Soups and Salad

Mixed Greens Salad with Grilled Chicken

Cooking Time: 15-20 mins   **Preparation Time:** 15 mins   **Servings:** 2

Ingredients:
- 2 cups mixed salad greens
- 4 ounces grilled chicken breast, sliced
- 1/4 cup cherry tomatoes, halved
- 1/4 cup cucumber, sliced
- 1/4 cup red onion, thinly sliced
- 1 tablespoon extra-virgin olive oil
- 1 tablespoon balsamic vinegar
- Pepper and salt to taste

Instructions:
1. Combine the mixed salad greens, grilled chicken slices, cherry tomatoes, cucumber, and red onion in a large bowl.
2. Whisk together the extra virgin olive oil and balsamic vinegar in a small bowl.
3. Drizzle the dressing over the salad and toss to combine.
4. Season with pepper and salt to taste.
5. Serve immediately.

Nutrition Facts:
Per serving: Calories: 280 kcal, Carbs: 9 g, Proteins: 28 g, Fats: 15 g

Lentil Soup

Cooking Time: 30-40 mins   **Preparation Time:** 15 mins   **Servings:** 2

Ingredients:
- 1 cup dry lentils, rinsed
- 4 cups low-sodium vegetable broth
- 1 medium onion, chopped
- 2 medium carrots, chopped
- 2 stalks of celery, chopped
- 2 cloves garlic, minced
- 1 teaspoon cumin
- 1/2 teaspoon paprika
- Pepper and salt to taste

Instructions:
1. Combine the rinsed lentils, vegetable broth, onion, carrots, celery, garlic, cumin, paprika, salt, and pepper in a large pot.
2. Bring the mixture to a boil over medium heat, then reduce the heat to low and simmer for about 30 minutes or until the lentils are tender.
3. Adjust the seasonings if needed.
4. Ladle the soup into bowls and serve hot.

Nutrition Facts:
Per serving: Calories: 210 kcal, Carbs: 36 g, Proteins: 14 g, Fats: 1g

Spinach and Berry Salad

⏲ *Cooking Time: No*   🍳 *Preparation Time: 10 mins*   🍽 *Servings: 2*

Ingredients:

- *2 cups baby spinach*
- *1/2 cup strawberries, sliced*
- *1/4 cup blueberries*
- *2 tablespoons slivered almonds*
- *1 tablespoon feta cheese, crumbled*
- *1 tablespoon balsamic vinaigrette dressing*

Instructions:

1. Combine the baby spinach, sliced strawberries, blueberries, slivered almonds, and crumbled feta cheese in a large salad bowl.
2. Whisk together the balsamic vinaigrette dressing, olive oil, and lemon juice in a small bowl.
3. Drizzle the dressing over the salad and toss gently to coat.
4. Serve immediately.

Nutrition Facts:

Per serving: Calories: 180 kcal, Carbs: 15 g, Proteins: 4 g, Fats: 12g

Tomato Basil Soup

⏲ *Cooking Time: 30-40 mins*   🍳 *Preparation Time: 15 mins*   🍽 *Servings: 2*

Ingredients:

- *4 large tomatoes, diced*
- *1 onion, chopped*
- *2 cloves garlic, minced*
- *1 cup low-sodium vegetable broth*
- *1 tablespoon olive oil*
- *1/4 cup fresh basil, chopped*
- *Pepper and salt to taste*

Instructions:

1. In a large saucepan, heat the olive oil over medium heat.
2. Add the chopped onions, minced garlic, and sauté until they become translucent.
3. Add the diced tomatoes, vegetable broth, dried basil, salt, and pepper. Stir well.
4. Bring the mixture to a boil, then reduce the heat to low and simmer for about 20 minutes.
5. Remove the soup from the heat and let it cool slightly.
6. Use an immersion blender or a countertop blender to puree the soup until smooth.
7. Reheat the soup if needed, and adjust the seasonings to taste.
8. Serve hot, garnished with fresh basil leaves if desired.

Nutrition Facts:

Per serving: Calories: 130 kcal, Carbs: 18 g, Proteins: 3 g, Fats: 6 g

Quinoa and Vegetable Salad

Cooking Time: 15-20mins   *Preparation Time: 20 mins*   *Servings: 2*

Ingredients:

- *1 cup cooked quinoa*
- *1 cup mixed vegetables (such as bell peppers, zucchini, and cherry tomatoes), diced*
- *1/4 cup red onion, finely chopped*
- *2 tablespoons lemon juice*
- *1 tablespoon extra-virgin olive oil*
- *1 tablespoon fresh parsley, chopped*
- *Pepper and salt to taste*

Instructions:

1. Combine the cooked quinoa, mixed vegetables, red onion, lemon juice, extra virgin olive oil, parsley, salt, and pepper in a large bowl.
2. Toss gently to mix all the ingredients well.
3. Adjust the seasonings if needed.
4. Serve at room temperature or chilled.

Nutrition Facts:

Per serving: Calories: 220 Kcal, Carbs: 32 g, Proteins: 6 g, Fats: 8 g

Chicken Vegetable Soup

Cooking Time: 30-40 mins   *Preparation Time: 20 mins*   *Servings: 2*

Ingredients:

- *4 cups low-sodium chicken broth*
- *1 cup cooked chicken breast, shredded*
- *1 cup mixed vegetables (such as carrots, celery, and green beans), chopped*
- *1/4 cup onion, chopped*
- *2 cloves garlic, minced*
- *1 teaspoon dried thyme*
- *Pepper and salt to taste*

Instructions:

1. In a large pot, combine the chicken broth, cooked shredded chicken, chopped vegetables, chopped onion, minced garlic, dried thyme, salt, and pepper.
2. Bring the mixture to a boil over medium heat, then reduce the heat to low and simmer for about 20 minutes or until the vegetables are tender.
3. Adjust the seasonings if needed.
4. Ladle the soup into bowls and serve hot.

Nutrition Facts:

Per serving: Calories: 180 kcal, Carbs: 8 g, Proteins: 24 g, Fats: 6 g

The Diabetic Cookbook After 50

Greek Salad

Cooking Time: No *Preparation Time: 10 mins* *Servings: 2*

Ingredients:

- *2 cups romaine lettuce, chopped*
- *1/4 cup cucumber, diced*
- *1/4 cup cherry tomatoes, halved*
- *1/4 cup kalamata olives, pitted*
- *2 tablespoons feta cheese, crumbled*
- *1 tablespoon extra-virgin olive oil*
- *1 tablespoon lemon juice*
- *Pepper and salt to taste*

Instructions:

1. Combine the chopped romaine lettuce, diced cucumber, cherry tomatoes, kalamata olives, and crumbled feta cheese in a large salad bowl.
2. Whisk together the extra virgin olive oil,lemon juice, salt, and pepper in a small bowl.
3. Drizzle the dressing over the salad and toss gently to coat.
4. Serve immediately.

Nutrition Facts:

Per serving: Calories: 180 kcal, Carbs: 8 g, Proteins: 5 g, Fats: 15 g,

Minestrone Soup

Cooking Time: 40-50 mins *Preparation Time: 15 mins* *Servings: 2*

Ingredients:

- *4 cups low-sodium vegetable broth*
- *1 cup diced tomatoes*
- *1/2 cup kidney beans, drained and rinsed*
- *1/2 cup whole wheat pasta, cooked*
- *1/2 cup zucchini, diced*
- *1/4 cup onion, chopped*
- *2 cloves garlic, minced*
- *1 teaspoon dried Italian seasoning*
- *Pepper and salt to taste*

Instructions:

1. In a large pot, combine the vegetable broth, diced tomatoes, kidney beans, cooked pasta, diced zucchini, chopped onion, minced garlic, dried Italian seasoning, salt, and pepper.
2. Bring the mixture to a boil over medium heat, then reduce the heat to low and simmer for about 15 minutes or until the flavors meld together.
3. Adjust the seasonings if needed.
4. Ladle the soup into bowls and serve hot.

Nutrition Facts:

Per serving: Calories: 220 kcal, Carbs: 43 g, Proteins: 10 g, Fats: 2 g

Tuna Salad with Avocado

Cooking Time: No *Preparation Time: 10 mins* *Servings: 2*

Ingredients:

- *1 can (5 ounces) water-packed tuna, drained*
- *1/2 avocado, mashed*
- *2 tablespoons red bell pepper, diced*
- *2 tablespoons red onion, chopped*
- *1 tablespoon lemon juice*
- *Pepper and salt to taste*

Instructions:

1. Combine the drained tuna, mashed avocado, diced red bell pepper, chopped red onion, lemon juice, salt, and pepper in a bowl.
2. Mix well until all the ingredients are evenly incorporated.
3. Adjust the seasonings if needed.
4. Serve chilled on a bed of lettuce or as a sandwich filling.

Nutrition Facts:

Per serving: Calories: 230 Kcal, Carbs: 10 g, Proteins: 25 g, Fats: 11 g

Butternut Squash Soup

Cooking Time: 35-45 mins *Preparation Time: 15 mins* *Servings: 2*

Ingredients:

- *4 cups butternut squash, peeled and cubed*
- *1 medium onion, chopped*
- *2 cloves garlic, minced*
- *4 cups low-sodium vegetable broth*
- *1 tablespoon olive oil*
- *1/4 teaspoon ground cinnamon*
- *Pepper and salt to taste*

Instructions:

1. In a large pot, heat the olive oil over medium heat.
2. Add the chopped onions, minced garlic, and sauté until they become translucent.
3. Add the cubed butternut squash and cook for a few minutes.
4. Pour in the vegetable broth, cinnamon, salt, and pepper.
5. Bring the mixture to a boil, then reduce the heat to low and simmer for about 20-25 minutes or until the squash is tender.
6. Use an immersion blender or a countertop blender to puree the soup until smooth.
7. Reheat the soup if needed, and adjust the seasonings to taste.
8. Serve hot, garnished with a sprinkle of cinnamon if desired.

Nutrition Facts:

Per serving: Calories: 180 Kcal, Carbs: 33 g, Proteins: 4 g, Fats: 6 g

Roasted Beet and Orange Salad

⏱ **Cooking Time: 45-50mins**   ⚖ **Preparation Time: 10 mins**   🛎 **Servings: 2**

Ingredients:

- 3 medium beets, roasted and sliced
- 2 oranges, peeled and segmented
- 4 cups of arugula
- 1/4 cup crumbled feta cheese
- 1/4 cup chopped walnuts
- 2 tablespoons of balsamic vinegar
- 1 tablespoon of extra-virgin olive oil
- Pepper and salt to taste

Instructions:

1. Preheat the oven to 400°F (200°C). Wash the beets, wrap them in foil, and place them on a baking sheet. Roast in the oven for about 45 minutes or until tender when pierced with a fork. Let the beets cool, then peel and slice them.
2. In a large bowl, combine the roasted beet slices, orange segments, arugula, feta cheese, and walnuts.
3. In a small bowl, whisk together the balsamic vinegar, olive oil, salt, and pepper. Drizzle the dressing over the salad and toss gently to combine.
4. Serve the salad immediately.

Nutrition Facts:

Per serving: Calories: 212 kcal, Carbs: 18 g, Proteins: 7 g, Fats: 14g

Spinach and Feta Soup

⏱ **Cooking Time: 20-25 mins**   ⚖ **Preparation Time: 15 mins**   🛎 **Servings: 2**

Ingredients:

- 1 tablespoon of olive oil
- 1 small onion, diced
- 2 cloves of garlic, minced
- 4 cups low-sodium vegetable broth
- 1 package (10 ounces) of frozen spinach, thawed and drained
- 1/2 cup crumbled feta cheese
- 1/4 cup fresh dill, chopped
- Pepper and salt to taste

Instructions:

1. Heat the olive oil in a large pot over medium heat. Add the onion and garlic, and sauté until the onion is translucent.
2. Add the vegetable broth and bring to a boil.
3. Stir in the spinach, feta cheese, and fresh dill. Simmer for about 10 minutes.
4. Season with pepper and salt to taste.
5. Ladle the soup into bowls and serve.

Nutrition Facts:

Per serving: Calories: 120 kcal, Carbs: 9 g, Protein: 7 g, Fat: 7 g

Kale and Chickpea Soup

Cooking Time: 25mins   *Preparation Time: 10 mins*   *Servings: 2*

Ingredients:

- 1 tablespoon olive oil
- 1 medium onion, diced
- 2 cloves garlic, minced
- 2 carrots, peeled and chopped
- 2 celery stalks, chopped
- 4 cups low-sodium vegetable broth
- 1 can (14 ounces) diced tomatoes, undrained
- 1 can (15 ounces) chickpeas, drained and rinsed
- 1 teaspoon dried oregano
- 1/2 teaspoon dried thyme
- Pepper and salt to taste

Instructions:

1. Heat olive oil in a large pot over medium heat. Add onion, garlic, carrots, and celery. Sauté until the vegetables are tender, about 5 minutes.
2. Pour in the vegetable broth and diced tomatoes with their juices. Bring to a boil, then reduce heat and simmer for 10 minutes.
3. Add the chickpeas, kale, oregano, and thyme to the pot. Simmer for an additional 10 minutes or until the kale is wilted.
4. Season with pepper and salt to taste. Serve hot.

Nutrition Facts:

Per serving: Calories: 200 Kcal, Carbs: 32 g, Proteins: 10g Fats: 5 g

Mexican Quinoa Salad

Cooking Time: 15-20 mins   *Preparation Time: 15 mins*   *Servings: 2*

Ingredients:

- 1 cup of cooked quinoa
- 1 can (15 ounces) of black beans, rinsed and drained
- 1 cup cherry tomatoes, halved
- 1/2 cup red bell pepper, diced
- 1/2 cup corn kernels
- 1/4 cup red onion, finely chopped
- 1/4 cup fresh cilantro, chopped
- 1 tablespoon lime juice
- 1 tablespoon extra-virgin olive oil
- 1 teaspoon ground cumin
- Pepper and salt to taste
- Optional toppings: avocado slices, diced jalapeños, low-fat Greek yogurt

Instructions:

1. In a large bowl, combine the cooked quinoa, black beans, cherry tomatoes, red bell pepper, corn kernels, red onion, and cilantro.
2. In a small bowl, whisk together the lime juice, olive oil, ground cumin, salt, and pepper.
3. Pour the dressing over the salad and toss gently to combine.
4. Refrigerate for at least 1 hour before serving to allow the flavors to develop.
5. Serve with optional toppings, if desired.

Nutrition Facts:

Per serving: Calories: 222 Kcal, Carbs: 37 g, Proteins: 10 g, Fats: 5 g

The Diabetic Cookbook After 50

Chicken Tortilla Soup

Cooking Time: 30-40mins *Preparation Time: 20 mins* *Servings: 2*

Ingredients:

- *1 tablespoon of olive oil*
- *1 small onion, diced*
- *2 cloves of garlic, minced*
- *1 teaspoon ground cumin*
- *1/2 teaspoon chili powder*
- *4 cups low-sodium chicken broth*
- *1 can (14.5 ounces) diced tomatoes, undrained*
- *1 cup cooked chicken breast, shredded*
- *1/2 cup frozen corn kernels*
- *1/2 cup black beans, rinsed and drained*
- *Juice of 1 lime*
- *Pepper and salt to taste*
- *Fresh cilantro, chopped (for garnish)*
- *Baked tortilla chips (optional for serving)*

Instructions:

1. Heat olive oil in a large pot over medium heat. Add onion, garlic, carrots, and celery. Sauté until the vegetables are tender, about 5 minutes.
2. Pour in the vegetable broth and diced tomatoes with their juices. Bring to a boil, then reduce heat and simmer for 10 minutes.
3. Add the chickpeas, kale, oregano, and thyme to the pot. Simmer for an additional 10 minutes or until the kale is wilted.
4. Season with pepper and salt to taste. Serve hot.

Nutrition Facts:

Per serving: Calories: 232 kcal, Carbs: 23 g, Proteins: 20 g, Fats: 7 g

Chapter 6:

Fish and Sea Food

Baked Lemon Herb Salmon

⏲ **Cooking Time: 10 mins** 📖 **Preparation Time: 15-20mins** 🍳 **Servings: 2**

🛒 Ingredients:

- 4 salmon fillets (4-6 ounces each)
- 2 tablespoons fresh lemon juice
- 1 teaspoon dried dill
- 1 teaspoon dried thyme
- 1/2 teaspoon garlic powder
- Pepper and salt to taste

🥄 Instructions:

1. Preheat the oven to 400°F (200°C).
2. Place the salmon fillets on a baking sheet lined with parchment paper.
3. Drizzle the lemon juice over the fillets.
4. In a small bowl, mix together the dried dill, dried thyme, garlic powder, salt, and pepper.
5. Sprinkle the herb mixture evenly over the salmon fillets.
6. Bake in the preheated oven for about 12-15 minutes or until the salmon is cooked through and flakes easily with a fork.
7. Serve hot.

Nutrition Facts:
Per serving: Calories: 276 kcal Carbs: 34 g Protein: 14 g
Fat: 1g

Grilled Shrimp Skewers

⏲ **Cooking Time: 15 mins** 📖 **Preparation Time: 5-7 mins** 🍳 **Servings: 2**

🛒 Ingredients:

- 1-pound large shrimp, peeled and deveined
- 2 tablespoons olive oil
- 1 teaspoon smoked paprika
- 1/2 teaspoon garlic powder
- Pepper and salt to taste

🥄 Instructions:

1. Preheat the grill to medium-high heat.
2. In a bowl, combine the olive oil, smoked paprika, garlic powder, salt, and pepper.
3. Thread the shrimp onto skewers.
4. Brush the shrimp with the olive oil mixture.
5. Place the skewers on the preheated grill and cook for 2-3 minutes per side until the shrimp is pink and opaque.
6. Remove from the grill and serve hot.

Nutrition Fact:
Per serving: Calories: 162 kcal, Carbs: 1 g, Proteins: 24 g,
Fats: 6 g

Lemon Garlic Baked Salmon

Cooking Time: 5 mins *Preparation Time: 12-15mins* *Servings: 2*

Ingredients:

- *4 salmon fillets (4-6 ounces each)*
- *2 tablespoons fresh lemon juice*
- *2 cloves garlic, minced*
- *1 tablespoon olive oil*
- *1 teaspoon dried dill*
- *Pepper and salt to taste*
- *Lemon slices for garnish*

Instructions:

1. Preheat the oven to 375°F (190°C). Line a baking sheet with parchment paper.
2. Place the salmon fillets on the prepared baking sheet.
3. In a small bowl, whisk together the lemon juice, minced garlic, olive oil, dried dill, salt, and pepper.
4. Drizzle the lemon garlic mixture over the salmon fillets, ensuring they are evenly coated.
5. Bake in the preheated oven for 12-15 minutes or until the salmon is cooked through and flakes easily with a fork.
6. Serve the salmon hot, garnished with lemon slices.

Nutrition Facts:
 Per serving: Calories: 288 kcal, Carbs: 2 g, Proteins: 33 g, Fats: 15g

Tuna Salad Lettuce Wraps

Cooking Time: 15 mins *Preparation Time: 0 mins* *Servings: 2*

Ingredients:

- *2 cans tuna in water, drained*
- *1/4 cup diced celery*
- *1/4 cup diced red onion*
- *2 tablespoons plain Greek yogurt*
- *1 tablespoon lemon juice*
- *Pepper and salt to taste*
- *Lettuce leaves for wrapping*

Instructions:

1. In a bowl, combine the drained tuna, diced celery, diced red onion, Greek yogurt, lemon juice, salt, and pepper.
2. Mix well until all ingredients are evenly incorporated.
3. Spoon the tuna salad onto lettuce leaves.
4. Wrap the lettuce leaves around the tuna salad to form wraps.
5. Serve immediately.

Nutrition Facts:
 Per serving: Calories: 133 kcal, Carbs: 3 g, Proteins: 26 g, Fats: 1 g

Baked White Fish with Tomatoes and Olives

Cooking Time: 10 mins *Preparation Time: 15-20mins* *Servings: 2*

Ingredients:

- 4 white fish fillets (such as tilapia or halibut) (4-6 ounces each)
- 1 cup cherry tomatoes, halved
- 1/4 cup sliced black olives
- 2 tablespoons olive oil
- 1 tablespoon fresh lemon juice
- 1 teaspoon dried oregano
- Pepper and salt to taste

Instructions:

1. Preheat the oven to 400°F (200°C).
2. Place the white fish fillets in a baking dish.
3. In a small bowl, mix together the cherry tomatoes, sliced black olives, olive oil, lemon juice, dried oregano, salt, and pepper.
4. Pour the tomato and olive mixture over the white fish fillets.
5. Bake in the preheated oven for about 15-18 minutes or until the fish is cooked through and flakes easily with a fork.
6. Serve hot.

Nutrition Facts:

Per serving: Calories: 130 kcal, Carbs: 4.6g Proteins: 4.6 g, Fats: 2.9 g

Grilled Salmon with Avocado Salsa

Cooking Time: 15 mins *Preparation Time: 10-12 mins* *Servings: 2*

Ingredients:

- 4 salmon fillets (4-6 ounces each)
- 1 avocado, diced
- 1/2 cup diced tomatoes
- 1/4 cup diced red onion
- 2 tablespoons chopped cilantro
- 1 tablespoon lime juice
- Pepper and salt to taste

Instructions:

1. Preheat the grill to medium-high heat.
2. In a bowl, combine the diced avocado, diced tomatoes, diced red onion, chopped cilantro, lime juice, salt, and pepper to make the avocado salsa. Set aside.
3. Season the salmon fillets with pepper and salt.
4. Place the salmon fillets on the grill and cook for about 4-5 minutes per side, or until cooked through.
5. Remove the salmon from the grill and top each fillet with the avocado salsa.
6. Serve hot.

Nutrition Fact:

Per serving: Calories: 308 kcal, Carbs: 7 g Proteins: 34 g, Fats: 18 g

Garlic and Herb Baked Shrimp

Cooking Time: 10 mins *Preparation Time: 10-12mins* *Servings: 2*

Ingredients:

- *1-pound large shrimp, peeled and deveined*
- *2 tablespoons olive oil*
- *2 cloves garlic, minced*
- *1 tablespoon chopped fresh parsley*
- *1 teaspoon dried basil*
- *Pepper and salt to taste*

Instructions:

1. Preheat the oven to 400°F (200°C).
2. In a bowl, combine the olive oil, minced garlic, chopped parsley, dried basil, salt, and pepper.
3. Place the shrimp in a baking dish and pour the olive oil mixture over the shrimp.
4. Toss the shrimp to coat them evenly.
5. Bake in the preheated oven for about 8-10 minutes or until the shrimp is pink and cooked through.
6. Serve hot.

Nutrition Facts:
   Per serving: Calories: 168 kcal, Carbs: 0 g, Proteins: 24 g, Fats: 7g

Seared Scallops with Cauliflower Mash

Cooking Time: 10 mins *Preparation Time: 10 mins* *Servings: 2*

Ingredients:

- *1 pound sea scallops*
- *2 tablespoons olive oil*
- *1 head cauliflower, chopped*
- *2 tablespoons unsalted butter*
- *1/4 cup unsweetened almond milk*
- *Pepper and salt to taste*

Instructions:

1. Bring a large pot of salted water to a boil.
2. Add the chopped cauliflower to the boiling water and cook for about 8-10 minutes or until tender.
3. Drain the cauliflower and return it to the pot.
4. Add the butter and almond milk to the pot and mash the cauliflower until smooth and creamy.
5. Season with pepper and salt to taste.
6. Meanwhile, heat olive oil in a skillet over medium-high heat.
7. Pat the sea scallops dry and season with pepper and salt.
8. Add the scallops to the hot skillet and cook for about 2-3 minutes per side, or until browned and cooked through.
9. Serve the seared scallops over the cauliflower mash.

Nutrition Facts:
   Per serving: Calories: 282 kcal, Carbs: 10 g, Proteins: 25 g, Fats: 15 g

The Diabetic Cookbook After 50

Baked Lemon Dijon Tilapia

⏲ *Cooking Time: 12-15 mins*   🍽 *Preparation Time: 10 mins*   🔔 *Servings: 2*

Ingredients:

- *4 tilapia fillets (4-6 ounces each)*
- *2 tablespoons Dijon mustard*
- *1 tablespoon fresh lemon juice*
- *1 teaspoon dried thyme*
- *1/2 teaspoon garlic powder*
- *Pepper and salt to taste*

Instructions:

1. Preheat the oven to 400°F (200°C).
2. Place the tilapia fillets on a baking sheet lined with parchment paper.
3. In a small bowl, whisk together the Dijon mustard, lemon juice, dried thyme, garlic powder, salt, and pepper.
4. Spread the mustard mixture over the tilapia fillets.
5. Bake in the preheated oven for about 12-15 minutes or until the tilapia is cooked through and flakes easily with a fork.
6. Serve hot.

Nutrition Facts:
Per serving: Calories: 162 kcal, Carbos: 0 g, Protein: 34 g, Fats: 2 g

Grilled Lemon Herb Swordfish

⏲ *Cooking Time: 10-12 mins*   🍽 *Preparation Time: 10 mins*   🔔 *Servings: 2*

Ingredients:

- *4 swordfish steaks (4-6 ounces each)*
- *2 tablespoons fresh lemon juice*
- *1 tablespoon olive oil*
- *1 teaspoon dried basil*
- *1 teaspoon dried thyme*
- *Pepper and salt to taste*

Instructions:

1. Preheat the grill to medium-high heat.
2. In a small bowl, whisk together the fresh lemon juice, olive oil, dried basil, dried thyme, salt, and pepper.
3. Brush the lemon herb mixture over both sides of the swordfish steaks.
4. Place the swordfish steaks on the preheated grill and cook for about 4-5 minutes per side, or until cooked through.
5. Remove from the grill and serve hot.

Nutrition Facts:
Per serving: Calories: 243 kcal Carbs: 1 g Protein: 34 g Fat: 0 g

Steamed Asian Ginger White Fish

Cooking Time: 10-12 mins   *Preparation Time: 10 mins*   *Servings: 2*

Ingredients:

- *4 white fish fillets (such as tilapia or halibut) (4-6 ounces each)*
- *2 tablespoons reduced-sodium soy sauce*
- *1 tablespoon rice vinegar*
- *1 tablespoon grated ginger*
- *2 cloves garlic, minced*
- *1 teaspoon sesame oil*
- *1/4 cup sliced green onions*

Instructions:

1. In a small bowl, whisk together the reduced-sodium soy sauce, rice vinegar, grated ginger, minced garlic, and sesame oil.
2. Place the white fish fillets on a heatproof plate that fits inside a steamer basket.
3. Pour the soy sauce mixture over the white fish fillets.
4. Place the plate in the steamer basket.
5. Steam the white fish fillets for about 10-12 minutes or until cooked through.
6. Sprinkle with sliced green onions before serving.

Nutrition Facts:

Per serving: Calories: 140 kcal, Carbs: 5.6g, Proteins: 20 g, Fats: 3.9 g,

Grilled Lemon Garlic Halibut

Cooking Time: 10-12 mins   *Preparation Time: 10 mins*   *Servings: 2*

Ingredients:

- *4 halibut fillets (4-6 ounces each)*
- *2 tablespoons olive oil*
- *2 tablespoons lemon juice*
- *2 cloves garlic, minced*
- *1 teaspoon lemon zest*
- *1/2 teaspoon dried thyme*
- *1/2 teaspoon salt*
- *1/4 teaspoon black pepper*
- *Lemon wedges for serving*
- *Fresh parsley for garnish*

Instructions:

1. Preheat the grill to medium-high heat.
2. In a small bowl, whisk together olive oil, lemon juice, minced garlic, lemon zest, dried thyme, salt, and black pepper.
3. Place the halibut fillets in a shallow dish and pour the marinade over them, ensuring they are coated evenly. Let them marinate for 15-30 minutes.
4. Lightly oil the grill grates to prevent sticking.
5. Grill the halibut fillets for about 4-6 minutes per side until they are cooked through and easily flake with a fork.
6. Remove the grilled halibut from the heat and serve with lemon wedges.
7. Garnish with fresh parsley before serving.

Nutrition Facts:

Per serving: Calories: 242 kcal, Carbs: 1 g, Proteins: 36 g, Fats: 0 g

Blackened Cajun Shrimp Salad

Cooking Time: 10 mins *Preparation Time: 15 mins* *Servings: 2*

Ingredients:

- *1-pound large shrimp, peeled and deveined*
- *2 teaspoons paprika*
- *1 teaspoon dried thyme*
- *1 teaspoon dried oregano*
- *1 teaspoon garlic powder*
- *1 teaspoon onion powder*
- *1/2 teaspoon cayenne pepper (adjust according to spice preference)*
- *1/2 teaspoon salt*
- *1/4 teaspoon black pepper*
- *2 tablespoons olive oil*
- *8 cups mixed salad greens*
- *1 cup cherry tomatoes, halved*
- *1/2 cup sliced cucumber*
- *1/4 cup sliced red onion*
- *1/4 cup chopped fresh parsley*
- *Juice of 1 lemon*
- *Lemon wedges for serving*

Instructions:

1. In a small bowl, combine paprika, thyme, oregano, garlic powder, onion powder, cayenne pepper, salt, and black pepper to make the Cajun seasoning.
2. Heat olive oil in a large skillet over medium-high heat.
3. Pat the shrimp dry with paper towels and toss them in the Cajun seasoning to coat evenly.
4. Add the seasoned shrimp to the hot skillet and cook for 2-3 minutes per side until they turn pink and opaque. Be careful not to overcook.
5. In a large bowl, combine the salad greens, cherry tomatoes, cucumber, red onion, and chopped parsley.
6. Drizzle the salad with lemon juice and toss to combine.
7. Divide the salad among plates and top with the blackened Cajun shrimp.
8. Serve with lemon wedges on the side.

Nutrition Facts:

Per serving: Calories: 130 kcal, Carbs: 5.5g Proteins: 21 g Fats: 3.7g,

Baked Dijon Salmon

⏱ *Cooking Time: 15-20 mins*   ⏲ *Preparation Time: 10 mins*   🛎 *Servings: 2*

Ingredients:

- *4 salmon fillets (4-6 ounces each)*
- *2 tablespoons Dijon mustard*
- *2 tablespoons fresh lemon juice*
- *2 tablespoons olive oil*
- *1 tablespoon honey*
- *2 cloves garlic, minced*
- *1/2 teaspoon dried dill*
- *1/2 teaspoon salt*
- *Fresh dill for garnish*
- *Lemon wedges for serving*
- *Fresh dill for garnish*

Instructions:

1. Preheat the oven to 400°F (200°C).
2. In a small bowl, whisk together Dijon mustard, lemon juice, olive oil, honey, minced garlic, dried dill, salt, and black pepper.
3. Place the salmon fillets in a baking dish and brush the mustard mixture evenly over the top of each fillet.
4. Bake the salmon for about 12-15 mins, till it is cooked through and flakes easily with a fork.
5. Remove the baked salmon from the oven and let it rest for a few minutes before serving.
6. Serve with lemon wedges and garnish with fresh dill.

Nutrition Facts:

Per serving: Calories: 322 kcal, Carbs: 6 g, Fat: 18 g, Protein: 33 g

Broiled Lemon Garlic Swordfish

⏱ *Cooking Time: 10-12 mins*   ⏲ *Preparation Time: 10 mins*   🛎 *Servings: 2*

Ingredients:

- *4 swordfish steaks (4-6 ounces each)*
- *2 tablespoons olive oil*
- *2 tablespoons fresh lemon juice*
- *2 cloves garlic, minced*
- *1 teaspoon lemon zest*
- *1/2 teaspoon dried thyme*
- *1/2 teaspoon dried rosemary*
- *1/2 teaspoon salt*
- *1/4 teaspoon black pepper*
- *Lemon wedges for serving*
- *Fresh parsley for garnish*

Instructions:

1. Preheat the broiler to high heat.
2. In a small bowl, whisk together olive oil, lemon juice, minced garlic, lemon zest, dried thyme, dried rosemary, salt, and black pepper.
3. Place the swordfish steaks on a broiler pan or baking sheet lined with foil.
4. Brush the lemon garlic mixture over the swordfish steaks, coating them evenly.
5. Broil the swordfish for about 4-6 minutes per side or until it is cooked through and flakes easily with a fork.
6. Remove the broiled swordfish from the oven and let it rest for a few minutes before serving.
7. Serve with lemon wedges and garnish with fresh parsley.

Nutrition Facts:

Per serving: Calories: 291 kcal, Carbs: 0.5 g, Fats: 2 g, Proteins: 43 g

Thai Coconut Curry Shrimp

Cooking Time: 10-12 mins *Preparation Time: 15 mins* *Servings: 2*

Ingredients:

- *1-pound large shrimp, peeled and deveined*
- *1 tablespoon coconut oil*
- *1 onion, sliced*
- *2 bell peppers, sliced*
- *2 cloves garlic, minced*
- *1 tablespoon grated fresh ginger*
- *1 tablespoon Thai red curry paste*
- *1 can (13.5 ounces) of coconut milk*
- *1 tablespoon fish sauce*
- *1 tablespoon lime juice*
- *1 tablespoon chopped fresh cilantro (coriander)*
- *Salt, to taste*
- *Cooked brown rice for serving*
- *Fresh cilantro (coriander) leaves for garnish*

Instructions:

1. Heat coconut oil in a large skillet or wok over medium heat.
2. Add the sliced onion and bell peppers to the skillet and sauté for 3-4 minutes until they start to soften.
3. Add the minced garlic, grated ginger, and Thai red curry paste to the skillet. Stir and cook for another minute until fragrant.
4. Stir in the coconut milk, fish sauce, and lime juice. Bring the mixture to a simmer.
5. Add the shrimp to the skillet and cook for about 4-6 minutes until they are pink and cooked through.
6. Stir in the chopped cilantro and season with salt to taste.
7. Serve the Thai coconut curry shrimp over cooked brown rice.
8. Garnish with fresh cilantro leaves before serving.

Nutrition Facts:

Per serving: Calories: 238 kcal, Fats: 15 g, Carbs: 10 g, Proteins: 17 g

Greek Style Baked White Fish

Cooking Time: 15-20 mins   *Preparation Time: 10 mins*   *Servings: 2*

Ingredients:

- 4 white fish fillets (such as tilapia or halibut) (4-6 ounces each)
- 1 tablespoon olive oil
- 2 cloves garlic, minced
- 1 teaspoon dried oregano
- 1/2 teaspoon dried thyme
- 1/2 teaspoon dried basil
- 1/4 teaspoon black pepper
- 1 cup cherry tomatoes, halved
- 1/4 cup sliced black olives
- 1/4 cup crumbled feta cheese
- Fresh parsley for garnish

Instructions:

1. Preheat the oven to 400°F (200°C).
2. Place the white fish fillets in a baking dish lightly coated with olive oil.
3. In a small bowl, mix together olive oil, minced garlic, dried oregano, dried thyme, dried basil, salt, and black pepper.
4. Brush the herb mixture over the white fish fillets, coating them evenly.
5. Bake the white fish for about 12-15 mins, till it is cooked through and flakes easily with a fork.
6. Remove the baked white fish from the oven and let it rest for a few minutes before serving.
7. Garnish with fresh parsley before serving.

Nutrition Facts:

Per serving: Calories: 198 kcal, Carbs: 2.8 g, Proteins: 25 g, Fats: 10.8 g

Lemon Pepper Grilled Tuna Steaks

Cooking Time: 4-6 mins   *Preparation Time: 10 mins*   *Servings: 2*

Ingredients:

- 4 tuna steaks (4-6 ounces each)
- 2 tablespoons olive oil
- 2 tablespoons fresh lemon juice
- 1 teaspoon lemon zest
- 1 teaspoon freshly ground black pepper
- 1/2 teaspoon salt
- 1/2 teaspoon dried dill
- Lemon wedges for serving
- Fresh dill for garnish

Instructions:

1. Preheat the grill to medium-high heat.
2. In a small bowl, whisk together olive oil, lemon juice, lemon zest, black pepper, salt, and dried dill.
3. Place the tuna steaks in a shallow dish and pour the marinade over them, ensuring they are coated evenly. Let them marinate for 15-30 minutes.
4. Lightly oil the grill grates to prevent sticking.
5. Grill the tuna steaks for about 2-3 minutes per side until they are seared on the outside but still pink in the center.
6. Remove the grilled tuna from the heat and let them rest for a few minutes before serving.
7. Serve with lemon wedges and garnish with fresh dill.

Nutrition Facts:

Per serving: Calories: 241 Kcal, Carbs: 0.5 g, Proteins: 34 g, Fats: 11 g

Pesto Shrimp with Zucchini Noodles

Cooking Time: 10 mins *Preparation Time: 15 mins* *Servings: 2*

Ingredients:

- *1 pound large shrimp, peeled and deveined*
- *2 medium zucchini, spiralized or cut into thin noodles*
- *1/4 cup prepared pesto*
- *1 tablespoon olive oil*
- *2 cloves garlic, minced*
- *1/2 teaspoon red pepper flakes (optional)*
- *Salt, to taste*
- *Fresh basil leaves for garnish*

Instructions:

1. Heat olive oil in a large skillet over medium heat.
2. Add the minced garlic and red pepper flakes (if using) to the skillet. Sauté for about 1 minute until fragrant.
3. Add the shrimp to the skillet and cook for 2-3 minutes per side until they are pink and cooked through. Remove the shrimp from the skillet and set aside.
4. In the same skillet, add the zucchini noodles and cook for 2-3 minutes until they are tender-crisp. Avoid overcooking to prevent them from becoming mushy.
5. Return the shrimp to the skillet with the zucchini noodles.
6. Stir in the pesto sauce and toss everything together until well-coated. Cook for an additional 1-2 minutes to heat through.
7. Season with salt to taste.
8. Serve the pesto shrimp with zucchini noodles and garnish with fresh basil leaves.

Nutrition Facts:

Per serving: Calories: 206 kcal, Carbs: 5 g, Proteins: 21g
Fat: 12 g

Baked Parmesan Crusted Haddock

Cooking Time: 15-20 mins *Preparation Time: 10 mins* *Servings: 2*

Ingredients:

- *4 haddock fillets (4-6 ounces each)*
- *1/4 cup grated Parmesan cheese*
- *2 tablespoons almond flour (or whole wheat breadcrumbs)*
- *1 teaspoon dried parsley*
- *1/2 teaspoon dried oregano*
- *1/2 teaspoon paprika*
- *1/4 teaspoon garlic powder*
- *Lemon wedges for serving*
- *Fresh parsley for garnish*

Instructions:

1. Preheat the oven to 400°F (200°C).
2. In a shallow bowl, combine grated Parmesan cheese, almond flour (or breadcrumbs), dried parsley.
3. Press both sides of the haddock fillets into the Parmesan mixture, pressing lightly to adhere to the coating.
4. Place the coated haddock fillets on a baking sheet lined with parchment paper or foil.
5. Remove the baked haddock from the oven and let it rest for a few minutes before serving.
6. Serve with lemon wedges and garnish with fresh parsley.

Nutrition Facts:

Per serving: Calories: 243 kcal, Carbs: 2 g, Proteins: 27g
Fats: 13 g

Shrimp and Avocado Salad

Cooking Time: No *Preparation Time: 15 mins* *Servings: 2*

Ingredients:

- *1-pound cooked shrimp, peeled and deveined*
- *2 avocados, diced*
- *1 cup cherry tomatoes, halved*
- *1/4 cup red onion, thinly sliced*
- *1/4 cup chopped fresh cilantro (coriander)*
- *2 tablespoons lime juice*
- *2 tablespoons olive oil*
- *1 clove garlic, minced*
- *1/2 teaspoon ground cumin*
- *Salt and black pepper, to taste*
- *Mixed salad greens for serving*

Instructions:

1. In a large bowl, combine cooked shrimp, diced avocados, cherry tomatoes, red onion, and chopped cilantro.
2. In a small bowl, whisk together lime juice, olive oil, minced garlic, ground cumin, salt, and black pepper to make the dressing.
3. Pour the dressing over the shrimp and avocado mixture. Toss gently to coat everything evenly.
4. Refrigerate the shrimp and avocado salad for at least 30 minutes to allow the flavors to meld.
5. Serve the chilled salad on a bed of mixed salad greens.

Nutrition Facts:

Per serving: Calories: 28 Kcal, Carbs 7 g, Proteins: 20 g Fats: 19 g,

Chapter 7:

Poultry and Meat

Grilled Lemon Herb Chicken

⏲ *Cooking Time: 15-20* 🍳 *Preparation Time: 10 mins* 🔔 *Servings: 2*

🛒 Ingredients:
- *4 boneless, skinless chicken breasts*
- *2 tablespoons olive oil*
- *1 tablespoon lemon juice*
- *1 teaspoon dried herbs (such as thyme, rosemary, or oregano)*

🍴 Instructions:
1. Preheat the grill to medium-high heat.
2. Combine olive oil, lemon juice, and dried herbs in a small bowl.
3. Season chicken breasts with pepper and salt, then brush the herb mixture over both sides.
4. Grill chicken for about 6-8 minutes per side or until cooked through.
5. Serve hot.

Nutrition Facts:
Per serving: Calories: 220 kcal, Carbs: 0 g, Proteins: 28 g, Fats: 11 g

Turkey Meatballs with Zucchini Noodles

⏲ *Cooking Time: 20-25 mins* 🍳 *Preparation Time: 20 mins* 🔔 *Servings: 2*

🛒 Ingredients:
- *1 lb. ground turkey*
- *1/4 cup almond flour*
- *1/4 cup grated Parmesan cheese*
- *1 teaspoon garlic powder*
- *2 zucchinis, spiralized*
- *1 cup marinara sauce (sugar-free)*

🍴 Instructions:
1. Preheat oven to 400°F (200°C).
2. Combine ground turkey, almond flour, Parmesan cheese, garlic powder, salt, and pepper in a bowl. Mix well.
3. Shape the mixture into meatballs of your desired size and place them on a baking sheet.
4. Bake for about 20-25 minutes or until cooked through.
5. While the meatballs are baking, spiralize the zucchini to make noodles.
6. Heat a non-stick pan over medium heat and sauté the zucchini noodles for a few minutes until tender.
7. Topped with marinara sauce, serve the turkey meatballs on top of the zucchini noodles.

Nutrition Facts:
Per serving: Calories: 290 kcal, Carbs: 10 g, Proteins: 28 g, Fats: 16 g

Herb-Roasted Chicken Breast with Vegetables

Cooking Time: 25-30 mins **Preparation Time:** 10 mins **Servings:** 2

Ingredients:

- *4 boneless, skinless chicken breasts*
- *2 tablespoons olive oil*
- *1 teaspoon dried rosemary*
- *1 teaspoon dried thyme*
- *1 teaspoon dried oregano*
- *1/2 teaspoon garlic powder*
- *Pepper and salt to taste*
- *2 cups mixed vegetables (such as bell peppers, zucchini, and carrots), cut into bite-sized pieces*

Instructions:

1. Preheat the oven to 400°F (200°C). Grease a baking dish with olive oil or line it with parchment paper.
2. Place the chicken breasts in the baking dish. Drizzle with olive oil and sprinkle with dried rosemary, dried thyme, dried oregano, garlic powder, salt, and pepper. Rub the herbs and spices onto the chicken to coat evenly.
3. Arrange the mixed vegetables around the chicken breasts.
4. Bake in the preheated oven for 25-30 minutes or until the chicken is cooked through and the vegetables are tender.
5. Remove from the oven and let it rest for a few minutes before serving. Serve the herb-roasted chicken breast with the roasted vegetables.

Nutrition Facts:

Per serving: Calories: 236 Kcal, Carbs: 6 g Proteins: 33 g, Fats: 9 g,

Grilled Herb-Marinated Turkey Tenderloin

Cooking Time: 15-20 mins **Preparation Time:** 10mins **Servings:** 2

Ingredients:

- *2 turkey tenderloins (about 1 pound total)*
- *2 tablespoons balsamic vinegar*
- *2 tablespoons olive oil*
- *2 cloves garlic, minced*
- *1 teaspoon dried thyme*
- *1 teaspoon dried rosemary*
- *Pepper and salt to taste*

Instructions:

1. Preheat the grill to medium-high heat.
2. In a small bowl, whisk together the balsamic vinegar, olive oil, minced garlic, dried thyme, dried rosemary, salt, and pepper.
3. Place the turkey tenderloins in a shallow dish and pour the marinade over them, turning to coat evenly. Let them marinate for at least 30 minutes.
4. Remove the turkey tenderloins from the marinade and discard the excess marinade.
5. Grill the turkey tenderloins for about 15-20 minutes, turning occasionally, until they reach an internal temperature of 165°F (74°C).
6. Remove from the grill and let the turkey tenderloins rest for a few minutes before slicing. Serve hot.

Nutrition Facts:

Per serving: Calories: 178kcal, Carbs: 1g Proteins: 31g, Fats: 5,

Grilled Teriyaki Chicken Stir-Fry

Cooking Time: 10-12 mins *Preparation Time: 15 mins* *Servings: 2*

Ingredients:

- *4 boneless, skinless chicken breasts, sliced*
- *2 tablespoons low-sodium soy sauce*
- *1 tablespoon honey (or sugar substitute)*
- *1 tablespoon sesame oil*
- *Assorted vegetables (such as bell peppers, broccoli, and snap peas)*

Instructions:

1. Mix low-sodium soy sauce, honey (or sugar substitute), and sesame oil in a small bowl to make the teriyaki sauce.
2. Heat a grill pan or skillet over medium-high heat.
3. Grill or cook the chicken slices in the pan for about 6-8 minutes per side until cooked through.
4. Remove the chicken from the pan and set aside.
5. In the same pan, add the assorted vegetables and stir-fry until crisp-tender.
6. Return the chicken to the pan, pour the teriyaki sauce over the chicken and vegetables, and stir to coat.
7. Cook for an additional 2-3 minutes until heated through.
8. Serve hot.

Nutrition Facts:

Per serving: Calories: 250 kcal, Carbs: 10 g, Proteins: 30 g, Fats: 8 g

Oven-Roasted Turkey Breast

Cooking Time: 25 mins *Preparation Time: 15 mins* *Servings: 2*

Ingredients:

- *1 turkey breast (about 4 lbs.)*
- *2 tablespoons olive oil*
- *1 teaspoon dried sage*
- *1 teaspoon dried thyme*
- *Pepper and salt to taste*

Instructions:

1. Preheat oven to 350°F (175°C).
2. Rub the turkey breast with olive oil, dried sage, dried thyme, salt, and pepper.
3. Place the turkey breast on a roasting rack in a roasting pan.
4. Roast for about 20 minutes per pound or until the internal temperature reaches 165°F (74°C).
5. Remove from the oven and let it rest for a few minutes before slicing.
6. Serve hot.

Nutrition Facts:

Per serving: Calories: 180 kcal, Carbs: 0 g, Proteins: 40 g, Fats: 3 g

Grilled Balsamic Glazed Pork Chops

Cooking Time: 12-15mins   *Preparation Time: 10 mins*   *Servings: 2*

Ingredients:

- *4 boneless pork chops*
- *2 tablespoons balsamic vinegar*
- *1 tablespoon olive oil*
- *1 tablespoon Dijon mustard*

Instructions:

1. Preheat the grill to medium-high heat.
2. Whisk together balsamic vinegar, olive oil, Dijon mustard, salt, and pepper in a small bowl.
3. Brush the glaze over both sides of the pork chops.
4. Grill pork chops for about 4-5 minutes per side or until cooked through.
5. Serve hot

Nutrition Facts:
Per serving: Calories: 280 kcal, Carbs: 3 g, Proteins: 25 g, Fats: 16 g

Herb-Crusted Baked Chicken Thighs

Cooking Time: 30-35 mins   *Preparation Time: 10 mins*   *Servings: 2*

Ingredients:

- *4 oz. chicken*
- *2 tablespoons low-sodium soy sauce*
- *1 tablespoon cornstarch*
- *2 cloves garlic, minced*
- *1 teaspoon fresh ginger, grated*
- *2 cups broccoli florets*
- *1 red bell pepper, sliced*
- *1 tablespoon canola oil or olive oil*
- *Salt and black pepper to taste*

Instructions:

1. Preheat the oven to 400°F (200°C).
2. In a small bowl, whisk together the olive oil, Dijon mustard, dried thyme, dried rosemary, garlic powder, salt, and pepper.
3. Place the chicken thighs in a baking dish and brush the olive oil mixture all over them, making sure to cover them evenly.
4. Bake the chicken thighs in the preheated oven for about 30–35 mins, till the internal temperature reaches 165°F (74°C) and the skin is crispy.
5. Remove the chicken thighs from the oven and let them rest for a few minutes before serving.
6. Serve the herb-crusted chicken thighs with a side of roasted vegetables or a green salad.

Nutrition Facts:
Per serving: Calories: 330 kcal, Carbs: 1 g Proteins: 25 g, Fats: 24 g

Chicken and Broccoli Stir-Fry

Cooking Time: 12-15mins *Preparation Time: 10 mins* *Servings: 2*

Ingredients:

- *4 oz. chicken*
- *2 tablespoons low-sodium soy sauce*
- *1 tablespoon cornstarch*
- *2 cloves garlic, minced*
- *1 teaspoon fresh ginger, grated*
- *2 cups broccoli florets*
- *1 red bell pepper, sliced*
- *1 tablespoon canola oil or olive oil*
- *Salt and black pepper to taste*

Instructions:

1. In a small bowl, combine the low-sodium soy sauce, cornstarch, minced garlic, and grated ginger. Stir until the cornstarch is dissolved.
2. Place the chicken in a separate bowl and pour half of the soy sauce mixture over it. Toss to coat and let it marinate for 15 minutes.
3. Heat the canola oil or olive oil in a large skillet or wok over medium-high heat. Add the marinated chicken (reserve the marinade) and stir-fry for 3–4 minutes or until browned. Remove the chicken from the skillet and set it aside.
4. In the same skillet, add the broccoli florets and sliced red bell pepper. Stir-fry for 2–3 minutes or until the vegetables are crisp-tender.
5. Return the chicken to the skillet with the vegetables. Pour in the reserved marinade and cook for an additional 2 minutes or until the sauce has thickened.
6. Season with salt and black pepper to taste.
7. Serve the chicken and broccoli stir-fry over cauliflower rice or steamed brown rice.

Nutrition Facts:

Per serving: Calories: 359 kcal, Carbs: 38 g, Proteins: 29 g, Fats: 6.8 g

Chapter 8:

Desserts and Drinks

Sugar-Free Apple Crisp

⏱ *Cooking Time: 30-35 mins*   ⏲ *Preparation Time: 15 mins*   🔔 *Servings: 2*

Ingredients:

- *4 medium-sized apples, peeled and sliced*
- *1 cup rolled oats*
- *1/4 cup almond flour*
- *1/4 cup chopped walnuts*
- *1/4 cup melted coconut oil*
- *1/4 cup sugar substitute (such as stevia or erythritol)*
- *1 teaspoon cinnamon*
- *1/2 teaspoon nutmeg*

Instructions:

1. Preheat your oven to 350°F (175°C).
2. Combine the rolled oats, almond flour, chopped walnuts, melted coconut oil, sugar substitute, cinnamon, and nutmeg in a mixing bowl. Mix well.
3. Place the sliced apples in a baking dish and sprinkle the oat mixture evenly over the apples.
4. Bake for 30-35 minutes or until the apples are tender and the topping is golden brown.
5. Allow it to cool for a few minutes before serving.

Nutrition Facts:

Per serving: Calories: 160 kcal. Carbs: 23 g, Proteins: 3 g, Fats: 8 g

Chocolate Avocado Mousse

⏱ *Cooking Time: No*   ⏲ *Preparation Time: 10 mins*   🔔 *Servings: 2*

Ingredients:

- *2 ripe avocados*
- *1/4 cup unsweetened cocoa powder*
- *1/4 cup sugar substitute (such as stevia or erythritol)*
- *1/4 cup unsweetened almond milk*
- *1 teaspoon vanilla extract*

Instructions:

1. Cut the avocados in half, remove the pits, and scoop out the flesh into a blender or food processor.
2. Add the cocoa powder, sugar substitute, almond milk, and vanilla extract to the blender.
3. Blend until the mixture is smooth and creamy.
4. Transfer the mousse to serving bowls or glasses.
5. Refrigerate for at least 1 hour before serving. Garnish with shaved dark chocolate if desired. Enjoy!

Nutrition Facts:

Per serving: Calories: 150 kcal, Carbs: 9 g, Proteins: 3 g, Fats: 14 g

Low-Carb Berry Chia Pudding

⏱ **Cooking Time: 4 hours**   🍲 **Preparation Time: 5 mins**   🛎 **Servings: 2**

Ingredients:

- 1 cup unsweetened almond milk
- 1/4 cup chia seeds
- 1 tablespoon sugar substitute (such as stevia or erythritol)
- 1/2 teaspoon vanilla extract
- 1/2 cup mixed berries (e.g., strawberries, blueberries, raspberries)

Instructions:

1. Combine the almond milk, chia seeds, sugar substitute, and vanilla extract in a bowl.
2. Stir well to ensure the chia seeds are evenly distributed.
3. Cover the bowl and refrigerate for at least 2 hours or overnight, allowing the chia seeds to expand and thicken the mixture.
4. Before serving, give the pudding a good stir to break up any clumps that may have formed.
5. Top with mixed berries and enjoy!

Nutrition Facts:

Per serving: Calories: 120 kcal, Carbs: 10 g, Proteins: 4 g, Fats: 6 g

Sugar-Free Banana Bread

⏱ **Cooking Time: 55-60 mins**   🍲 **Preparation Time: 15 mins**   🛎 **Servings: 2**

Ingredients:

- 3 ripe bananas, mashed
- 2 cups almond flour
- 1/4 cup coconut flour
- 1/4 cup sugar substitute (such as stevia or erythritol)
- 3 large eggs
- 1/4 cup unsweetened almond milk
- 1 teaspoon baking powder
- 1/2 teaspoon baking soda
- 1/2 teaspoon cinnamon
- 1/4 teaspoon salt

Instructions:

1. Preheat your oven to 350°F (175°C). Grease a loaf pan or line it with parchment paper.
2. Combine the mashed bananas, almond flour, coconut flour, sugar substitute, eggs, almond milk, baking powder, baking soda, cinnamon, and salt in a large mixing bowl. Mix well until the batter is smooth.
3. Pour the batter into the prepared loaf pan and smooth the top with a spatula.
4. Bake for 45-50 minutes or until a toothpick inserted into the center comes out clean.
5. Remove from the oven and let it cool in the pan for 10 minutes. Then, transfer the bread to a wire rack to cool completely. Slice and enjoy!

Nutrition Facts:

Per serving: Calories: 160 kcal, Carbs: 15 g, Proteins: 4 g, Fats: 10g

Greek Yogurt Parfait

Cooking Time: 15 mins *Preparation Time: 10 mins* *Servings: 2*

Ingredients:

- 2 cups almond flour
- 1/4 cup coconut flour
- 1/4 cup sugar substitute (such as stevia or erythritol)
- 1/2 cup unsalted butter, softened
- 1 large egg
- 1 teaspoon vanilla extract
- 1/2 teaspoon baking soda
- 1/4 teaspoon salt
- 1/2 cup sugar-free chocolate chips

Instructions:

1. Preheat your oven to 350°F (175°C). Line a baking sheet with parchment paper.
2. Combine the almond flour, coconut flour, sugar substitute, softened butter, egg, vanilla extract, baking soda, and salt in a mixing bowl. Mix well until a dough forms.
3. Fold in the sugar-free chocolate chips until they are evenly distributed throughout the dough.
4. Use a tablespoon or cookie scoop to drop rounded dough portions onto the prepared baking sheet. Flatten each dough portion slightly with the back of a spoon or your fingers.
5. Bake for 12-15 minutes or until the edges turn golden brown.
6. Allow the cookies to cool on the baking sheet for a few minutes before transferring them to a wire rack to cool completely. Enjoy!

Nutrition Fact:
Per serving: Calories: 180 kcal, Carbs: 20 g, Proteins: 15 g, Fats: 6 g

Cinnamon Pear Crumble

Cooking Time: 30 mins *Preparation Time: 15 mins* *Servings: 2*

Ingredients:

- 4 ripe pears, peeled and sliced
- 1 tablespoon lemon juice
- 1/2 cup almond flour
- 1/2 cup rolled oats
- 1/4 cup chopped walnuts
- 2 tablespoons unsalted butter, melted
- 1 tablespoon honey or a sugar substitute
- 1 teaspoon ground cinnamon
- 1/4 teaspoon salt

Instructions:

1. Preheat the oven to 350°F (175°C).
2. In a bowl, toss the sliced pears with lemon juice to prevent browning.
3. Arrange the pear slices evenly in a baking dish.
4. In a separate bowl, combine almond flour, rolled oats, chopped walnuts, melted butter, honey or sugar substitute, cinnamon, and salt. Mix well until the mixture resembles coarse crumbs.
5. Bake for about 30 minutes or until the topping is golden brown and the pears are tender.
6. Remove from the oven and let it cool for a few minutes.
7. Serve warm or at room temperature. You can enjoy it as is or pair it with a scoop of sugar-free vanilla ice cream or a dollop of Greek yogurt.

Nutrition Facts:
Per serving: Calories: 210 kcal, Carbs: 24 g, Proteins: 3g, Fats: 13 g

The Diabetic Cookbook After 50

Sugar-Free Coconut Macaroons

Cooking Time: 15-20mins *Preparation Time: 15 mins* *Servings: 2*

Ingredients:
- *2 cups unsweetened shredded coconut*
- *1/2 cup sugar substitute (such as stevia or erythritol)*
- *4 large egg whites*
- *1/2 teaspoon vanilla extract*
- *Pinch of salt*

Instructions:
1. Preheat your oven to 325°F (163°C). Line a baking sheet with parchment paper.
2. In a mixing bowl, combine the shredded coconut and sugar substitute. Mix well.
3. In a separate bowl, whisk the egg whites until frothy.
4. Add the vanilla extract and salt to the frothy egg whites and continue whisking until soft peaks form.
5. Drop spoonfuls of the mixture onto the prepared baking sheet, shaping them into small mounds.
6. Bake for 20-25 minutes or until the macaroons turn golden brown.
7. Allow them to cool completely before removing them from the baking sheet. Enjoy!

Nutrition Facts:
Per serving: Calories: 120 kcal, Carbs: 8 g, Proteins: 3 g, Fats: 9 g

Coconut Chia Seed Popsicles

Cooking Time: 6 hours *Preparation Time: 10 mins* *Servings: 2*

Ingredients:
- *1 can (13.5 oz) coconut milk (full fat)*
- *2 tablespoons chia seeds*
- *2 tablespoons unsweetened shredded coconut*
- *1/4 teaspoon vanilla extract*
- *Optional: sugar substitute to taste*

Instructions:
1. In a bowl, whisk together coconut milk, chia seeds, shredded coconut, and vanilla extract.
2. Add sugar substitute if desired for additional sweetness.
3. Pour the mixture into popsicle molds.
4. Insert popsicle sticks and freeze for at least 4 hours or until completely solid.
5. Remove from molds and enjoy.

Nutrition Facts:
Per serving: Calories: 120 kcal, Carbs: 4 g, Proteins: 2 g, Fats: 11 g

Iced Green Tea with Lemon and Mint

Cooking Time: 10 mins *Preparation Time: 5 mins* *Servings: 2*

Ingredients:
- *2 green tea bags*
- *4 cups water*
- *1 lemon, sliced*
- *Fresh mint leaves*
- *Optional: sugar substitute to taste*

Instructions:
1. Bring water to a boil in a pot.
2. Remove from heat and add green tea bags.
3. Let the tea steep for about 3-5 minutes.
4. Remove the tea bags and let the tea cool to room temperature.
5. Add lemon slices and fresh mint leaves to the tea.
6. Refrigerate until chilled.
7. Serve over ice and enjoy.

Nutrition Facts:
Per serving: Calories: 5 kcal Carbs: 1 g Proteins: 0 g Fats: 0 g

Sparkling Berry Infused Water

Cooking Time: No *Preparation Time: 5 mins* *Servings: 2*

Ingredients:
- *1 cup mixed berries (strawberries, blueberries, raspberries)*
- *4 cups sparkling water*
- *Ice cubes*
- *Optional: sugar substitute to taste*

Instructions:
1. In a pitcher, combine mixed berries and sparkling water.
2. Add ice cubes.
3. Optionally, add sugar substitute for added sweetness.
4. Stir gently to combine.
5. Allow the flavors to infuse for about 10-15 minutes.
6. Serve chilled.

Nutrition Facts:
Per serving: Calories: 15 kcal, Carbs: 4 g, Proteins: 0 g, Fats: 0 g

Pumpkin Spice Smoothie

Cooking Time: No *Preparation Time: 5 mins* *Servings: 2*

Ingredients:

- *1/2 cup canned pumpkin (unsweetened)*
- *1/2 cup unsweetened almond milk*
- *1/2 cup plain Greek yogurt*
- *1 tablespoon almond butter*
- *1/2 teaspoon pumpkin spice*
- *Optional: sugar substitute to taste*

Instructions:

1. In a blender, combine canned pumpkin, almond milk, Greek yogurt, almond butter, pumpkin spice, and sugar substitute if desired.
2. Blend until smooth and creamy.
3. Pour into a glass and serve chilled.
4. Optionally, sprinkle some additional pumpkin spice on top for garnish.

Nutrition Facts:
Per serving: Calories: 140 kcal, Carbs: 12 g, Proteins: 9 g, Fats: 7 g

Almond Flour Blueberry Muffins

Cooking Time: 25-30 mins *Preparation Time: 15 mins* *Servings: 2*

Ingredients:

- *2 cups almond flour*
- *1/4 cup sugar substitute (stevia or erythritol)*
- *1/2 teaspoon baking powder*
- *1/4 teaspoon salt*
- *1/4 cup unsalted butter, melted*
- *2 large eggs*
- *1/4 cup unsweetened almond milk*
- *1 teaspoon vanilla extract*
- *1/2 cup fresh blueberries*

Instructions:

1. Preheat the oven to 350°F (175°C) and line a muffin tin with paper liners.
2. In a mixing bowl, combine almond flour, sugar substitute, baking powder, and salt.
3. In a separate bowl, whisk together melted butter, eggs, almond milk, and vanilla extract.
4. Gradually add the wet ingredients to the dry ingredients and stir until well combined.
5. Gently fold in the fresh blueberries.
6. Spoon the batter into the muffin cups, filling them about 3/4 full.
7. Bake for 20-25 minutes or until a toothpick inserted into the center comes out clean.
8. Allow the muffins to cool for a few minutes before transferring them to a wire rack to cool completely.

Nutrition Facts:
Per serving: Calories: 200 kcal, Carbs: 7 g, Proteins: 7 g, Fats: 18 g

Cucumber Mint Cooler

Cooking Time: No   *Preparation Time:* 5 mins   *Servings:* 2

Ingredients:
- *1/2 cup canned pumpkin (unsweetened)*
- *1/2 cup unsweetened almond milk*
- *1/2 cup plain Greek yogurt*
- *1 tablespoon almond butter*
- *1/2 teaspoon pumpkin spice*
- *Optional: sugar substitute to taste*

Instructions:
1. In a pitcher, combine cucumber slices, mint leaves, and water.
2. Optionally, add sugar substitute for added sweetness.
3. Stir well to infuse the flavors.
4. Refrigerate until chilled.
5. Serve over ice cubes and garnish with additional cucumber slices or mint leaves if desired.

Nutrition Facts:
Per serving: Calories: 10 kcal, Carbs: 2 g, Proteins: 0 g, Fats: 0 g

Chapter 9:

Meatless Main Dishes

Lentil and Vegetable Stir-Fry

Cooking Time: 20-25 mins   *Preparation Time: 10 mins*   *Servings: 2*

Ingredients:

- *1 cup cooked lentils*
- *2 cups mixed vegetables (bell peppers, broccoli, carrots, snow peas)*
- *2 cloves garlic, minced*
- *1 tablespoon low-sodium soy sauce*
- *1 tablespoon olive oil*

Instructions:

1. Heat olive oil in a skillet over medium heat.
2. Add garlic and sauté for 1 minute.
3. Add mixed vegetables and cook for 5 minutes, until slightly tender.
4. Stir in cooked lentils and soy sauce.
5. Cook for an additional 2 minutes, stirring occasionally.
6. Serve hot.

Nutrition Fact:
Per serving: Calories: 220 kcal, Carbs: 35 g, Proteins: 14 g, Fats: 4 g

Vegetable Stir-Fry

Cooking Time: 10-12 mins   *Preparation Time: 15 mins*   *Servings: 2*

Ingredients:

- *2 tablespoons low-sodium soy sauce*
- *1 tablespoon sesame oil*
- *2 cups mixed vegetables (such as bell peppers, carrots, snow peas, and broccoli)*
- *1 tablespoon olive oil*

Instructions:

1. In a small bowl, whisk together low-sodium soy sauce and sesame oil.
2. Heat a large skillet or wok over high heat.
3. In the same pan, add 1 tablespoon of olive oil and heat it.
4. Add the mixed vegetables to the pan and stir-fry for about 3-4 minutes until crisp-tender.
5. Pour the soy sauce mixture over the vegetables, and stir to coat.
6. Cook for an additional 2-3 minutes until heated through.
7. Serve hot.

Nutrition Facts:
Per serving: Calories: 360 kcal, Carbs: 10 g, Proteins: 1g, Fats: 5 g

Eggplant Parmesan

⏰ *Cooking Time: 30-35 mins* 🍳 *Preparation Time: 20 mins* 🔔 *Servings: 2*

Ingredients:

- *1 large eggplant, sliced into rounds*
- *1 cup whole wheat bread crumbs*
- *1/2 cup grated Parmesan cheese*
- *2 cups marinara sauce (low-sugar option)*
- *1/2 cup shredded mozzarella cheese*
- *1 tablespoon olive oil*
- *1 teaspoon dried basil*
- *Pepper and salt to taste*

Nutrition Fact:

Per serving: Calories: 250kcal, Carbs: 30 g, Proteins: 12 g, Fats: 10 g

Instructions:

1. Preheat the oven to 400°F (200°C).
2. In a bowl, combine bread crumbs, Parmesan cheese, dried basil, salt, and pepper.
3. Dip each eggplant slice into the bread crumb mixture, coating both sides.
4. Heat olive oil in a skillet over medium heat.
5. Cook the breaded eggplant slices in the skillet until golden brown on both sides.
6. Place the cooked eggplant slices in a baking dish.
7. Pour marinara sauce over the eggplant slices and sprinkle shredded mozzarella cheese on top.
8. Bake for 20 minutes, until the cheese is melted and bubbly.
9. Serve hot.

Chickpea Curry

⏰ *Cooking Time: 25-30 mins* 🍳 *Preparation Time: 15 mins* 🔔 *Servings: 2*

Ingredients:

- *1 can (15 ounces) chickpeas, rinsed and drained*
- *1 can (14 ounces) diced tomatoes*
- *1 onion, diced*
- *2 cloves garlic, minced*
- *1 tablespoon curry powder*
- *1 teaspoon cumin*
- *1 teaspoon turmeric*
- *1 teaspoon paprika*
- *1 tablespoon olive oil*
- *1 cup vegetable broth*
- *Pepper and salt to taste*
- *Fresh cilantro for garnish (optional)*

Instructions:

1. Heat olive oil in a skillet over medium heat.
2. Add onion and garlic, and sauté until translucent.
3. Stir in curry powder, cumin, turmeric, and paprika, cooking for 1 minute.
4. Add chickpeas, diced tomatoes, and vegetable broth.
5. Season with pepper and salt.
6. Reduce heat to low and simmer for 15 minutes, stirring occasionally.
7. Garnish with fresh cilantro, if desired.
8. Serve over brown rice or with whole wheat naan bread.

Nutrition Facts:

Per serving: Calories: 260 kcal, Carbs: 40 g, Proteins: 10 g, Fats: 7 g

Quinoa Stuffed Bell Peppers

Cooking Time: 25-30 mins *Preparation Time: 15 mins* *Servings: 2*

Ingredients:

- 4 large bell peppers (any color)
- 1 cup quinoa
- 1 tablespoon olive oil
- 1 small onion, diced
- 2 cloves garlic, minced
- 1 cup diced tomatoes (canned or fresh)
- 1 cup canned black beans, rinsed and drained
- 1 teaspoon cumin
- 1 teaspoon paprika
- Pepper and salt to taste
- 1/4 cup grated low-fat cheese (optional)
- Fresh parsley, chopped (for garnish)

Instructions:

1. Preheat the oven to 375°F (190°C). Cut off the tops of the bell peppers and remove the seeds and membranes. Place them in a baking dish and set aside.
2. Cook quinoa according to package instructions and set aside.
3. In a large skillet, heat olive oil over medium heat. Add diced onion and minced garlic, and sauté until softened and fragrant.
4. Add diced tomatoes, black beans, cumin, paprika, salt, and pepper to the skillet. Cook for 5 minutes, stirring occasionally.
5. Stir in cooked quinoa and mix well. Adjust seasoning if needed.
6. Spoon the quinoa mixture into the bell peppers, filling them to the top. If desired, sprinkle grated cheese over the stuffed peppers.
7. Cover the baking dish with foil and bake for 25-30 mins, till the peppers are tender and the filling is heated through.
8. Remove from the oven and garnish with chopped parsley before serving.

Nutrition Facts:

Per serving: Calories: 274 kcal, Carbs: 45 g, Proteins: 10 g, Fats: 6 g

Lentil and Vegetable Casserole

Cooking Time: 35-40 mins *Preparation Time: 15-20 mins* *Servings: 2*

Ingredients:

- *1 cup dried green or brown lentils*
- *2 tablespoons olive oil*
- *1 onion, chopped*
- *2 cloves garlic, minced*
- *2 carrots, diced*
- *2 celery stalks, diced*
- *1 red bell pepper, diced*
- *1 zucchini, diced*
- *1 can (14 oz) diced tomatoes*
- *1 teaspoon dried oregano*
- *1 teaspoon dried basil*
- *Pepper and salt to taste*
- *1/4 cup grated Parmesan cheese (optional)*

Instructions:

1. Cook lentils according to package instructions, then drain and set aside.
2. Preheat the oven to 375°F (190°C).
3. In a large skillet, heat olive oil over medium heat. Add chopped onion and minced garlic, and sauté until the onion becomes translucent.
4. Add diced carrots, celery, bell pepper, and zucchini to the skillet. Cook for about 5 minutes, until the vegetables start to soften.
5. Stir in the diced tomatoes, dried oregano, dried basil, salt, and pepper. Cook for another 5 minutes.
6. Transfer the cooked lentils to a large baking dish. Pour the vegetable mixture over the lentils and mix well.
7. Cover the baking dish with foil and bake for 25-30 mins, till the casserole is heated through.
8. If desired, sprinkle grated Parmesan cheese over the top and return to the oven for an additional 5 minutes to melt the cheese.
9. Serve hot as a satisfying meatless main dish.

Nutrition Facts:

Per serving: Calories: 248 kcal, Carbs: 40 g, Proteins: 12 g Fats: 4g

Spinach and Chickpea Curry

Cooking Time: 20-25 mins *Preparation Time: 10-20 mins* *Servings: 2*

Ingredients:

- 2 tablespoons olive oil
- 1 onion, chopped
- 3 cloves garlic, minced
- 1 tablespoon grated ginger
- 2 teaspoons curry powder
- 1 teaspoon ground cumin
- 1 teaspoon ground coriander
- 1/2 teaspoon turmeric
- 1/4 teaspoon cayenne pepper (optional, adjust to taste)
- 1 can (14 oz) diced tomatoes
- 1 can (14 oz) chickpeas, rinsed and drained
- 1 cup vegetable broth
- 4 cups fresh spinach leaves
- Pepper and salt to taste
- Fresh cilantro, chopped (for garnish)

Instructions:

1. Heat olive oil in a large skillet or pot over medium heat. Add chopped onion and sauté until translucent.
2. Add minced garlic and grated ginger to the skillet and cook for another minute, stirring constantly.
3. In a small bowl, combine curry powder, ground cumin, ground coriander, turmeric, and cayenne pepper (if using). Stir the spice mixture into the skillet and cook for a minute to toast the spices.
4. Pour in the diced tomatoes and their juice, followed by the chickpeas and vegetable broth. Stir well to combine.
5. Bring the mixture to a simmer and cook for 10 minutes, allowing the flavors to meld together.
6. Add fresh spinach leaves to the skillet and stir until wilted. Season with pepper and salt to taste.
7. Remove from heat and garnish with fresh chopped cilantro before serving.
8. Serve the spinach and chickpea curry with whole grain rice or quinoa for a complete meal.
9. These recipes provide a variety of flavors and textures while adhering to the dietary restrictions of a diabetic patient over 50 years old. Enjoy!

Nutrition Facts:

Per serving: Calories: 222 kcal, Carbs: 30 g, Proteins: 8 g, Fats: 6g

Spinach and Feta Stuffed Portobello Mushrooms

Cooking Time: 15-20 mins *Preparation Time: 15 mins* *Servings: 2*

Ingredients:

- 4 large Portobello mushrooms
- 2 cups fresh spinach, chopped
- 1/2 cup crumbled feta cheese
- 1/4 cup diced red onion
- 2 cloves garlic, minced
- 2 tablespoons olive oil
- Pepper and salt to taste

Instructions:

1. Preheat the oven to 375°F (190°C).
2. Remove the stems from the Portobello mushrooms and clean the caps.
3. In a skillet, heat olive oil over medium heat.
4. Sauté spinach, red onion, and garlic until spinach is wilted.
5. Remove from heat and stir in crumbled feta cheese.
6. Season with pepper and salt.
7. Fill each Portobello mushroom cap with the spinach and feta mixture.
8. Place the stuffed mushrooms on a baking sheet and bake for 20 minutes, until mushrooms are tender.
9. Serve warm.

Nutrition Facts:

Per serving: Calories: 150kcal, Carbs: 9 g, Proteins: 8 g, Fats: 10 g

Tofu and Vegetable Stir-Fry

Cooking Time: 15-20 mins *Preparation Time: 15 mins* *Servings: 2*

Ingredients:

- 1 package (14 ounces) of firm tofu, drained and cubed
- 2 cups mixed vegetables (broccoli, bell peppers, carrots, snap peas)
- 2 cloves garlic, minced
- 2 tablespoons low-sodium soy sauce
- 1 tablespoon sesame oil
- 1 tablespoon cornstarch
- 1/4 cup vegetable broth
- 1 tablespoon olive oil

Instructions:

1. In a small bowl, whisk together soy sauce, sesame oil, cornstarch, and vegetable broth. Set aside.
2. Heat olive oil in a skillet over medium heat.
3. Add garlic and sauté for 1 minute.
4. Add mixed vegetables and cook for 5-7 minutes until slightly tender.
5. Add tofu cubes and cook for an additional 3 minutes.
6. Pour the sauce mixture over the tofu and vegetables, stirring well.
7. Cook for 2 minutes, until the sauce thickens.
8. Serve hot over brown rice or whole wheat noodles.

Nutrition Facts:

Per serving: Calories: 220 kcal, Carbs: 14 g, Proteins: 16 g, Fats: 12g

Zucchini Noodles with Tomato and Basil

Cooking Time: 10-12 mins **Preparation Time:** 15 mins **Servings:** 2

Ingredients:

- 2 large zucchini, spiralized or cut into thin strips
- 1 cup cherry tomatoes, halved
- 2 cloves garlic, minced
- 2 tablespoons olive oil
- 1/4 cup fresh basil leaves, chopped
- Pepper and salt to taste

Instructions:

1. Heat olive oil in a skillet over medium heat.
2. Add garlic and sauté for 1 minute.
3. Add cherry tomatoes and cook for 2-3 minutes until slightly softened.
4. Add zucchini noodles to the skillet and sauté for 2-3 minutes until tender.
5. Season with pepper and salt.
6. Remove from heat and stir in chopped basil leaves.
7. Serve immediately.

Nutrition Facts:

Per serving: Calories: 120 kcal , Carbs: 8 g, Proteins: 3g, Fats: 9g

Black Bean and Vegetable Enchiladas

Cooking Time: 30-35 mins **Preparation Time:** 15 mins **Servings:** 2

Ingredients:

- 8 whole wheat tortillas
- 1 can (15 ounces) of black beans, rinsed and drained
- 1 cup diced bell peppers
- 1 cup diced zucchini
- 1/2 cup diced onion
- 1 can (14 ounces) of low-sodium enchilada sauce
- 1 cup shredded low-fat cheese
- 1 tablespoon olive oil
- 1 teaspoon ground cumin
- 1 teaspoon chili powder
- Pepper and salt to taste

Instructions:

1. Preheat the oven to 375°F (190°C).
2. Heat olive oil in a skillet over medium heat.
3. Add diced bell peppers, zucchini, and onion. Sauté until slightly softened.
4. Stir in black beans, cumin, chili powder, salt, and pepper. Cook for an additional 2 minutes.
5. Warm the tortillas in the microwave or oven.
6. Spoon the vegetable and black bean mixture onto each tortilla and roll it up.
7. Place the rolled tortillas in a baking dish.
8. Pour enchilada sauce over the tortillas and sprinkle shredded cheese on top.
9. Bake for 20 minutes, until the cheese is melted and bubbly.
10. Serve hot.

Nutrition Facts:

Per serving: Calories: 270 kcal, Carbs: 37 g , Proteins: 12 g, Fats: 7 g

Cauliflower Fried Rice

Cooking Time: 10-12 mins *Preparation Time: 15 mins* *Servings: 2*

Ingredients:

- *1 small head of cauliflower, grated or processed into a rice-like texture*
- *1 cup mixed vegetables (peas, carrots, corn)*
- *1/2 cup diced bell peppers*
- *1/4 cup diced onion*
- *2 cloves garlic, minced*
- *2 tablespoons low-sodium soy sauce*
- *1 tablespoon olive oil*
- *2 eggs, beaten (optional for vegetarian option)*
- *Pepper and salt to taste*
- *Chopped green onions for garnish (optional)*

Instructions:

1. Heat olive oil in a large skillet or wok over medium heat.
2. Add garlic and sauté for 1 minute.
3. Add diced bell peppers and onion. Sauté until slightly softened.
4. Add mixed vegetables and cook for 3-4 minutes until tender.
5. Push the vegetables to one side of the skillet and add beaten eggs to the other side. Scramble the eggs until cooked through.
6. Add grated cauliflower rice to the skillet and stir well to combine with the vegetables.
7. Stir in soy sauce, salt, and pepper. Cook for an additional 2-3 minutes until heated through.
8. Garnish with chopped green onions, if desired.
9. Serve hot.

Nutrition Facts:

Per serving: Calories: 180 kcal, Carbs: 15 g, Proteins: 7 g, Fats: 10 g

Lentil and Sweet Potato Curry

Cooking Time: 30-35 mins *Preparation Time: 20 mins* *Servings: 2*

Ingredients:

- *1 cup dried red lentils*
- *2 cups peeled and diced sweet potatoes*
- *1 can (14 ounces) coconut milk (light option)*
- *1 can (14 ounces) diced tomatoes*
- *1 onion, diced*
- *2 cloves garlic, minced*
- *1 tablespoon curry powder*
- *1 teaspoon ground cumin*
- *1 teaspoon ground turmeric*
- *1 tablespoon olive oil*
- *Pepper and salt to taste*
- *Fresh cilantro for garnish (optional)*

Instructions:

1. Rinse the lentils under cold water.
2. In a large pot, heat olive oil over medium heat.
3. Add onion and garlic, and sauté until translucent.
4. Stir in curry powder, cumin, and turmeric. Cook for 1 minute.
5. Add diced sweet potatoes, lentils, coconut milk, and diced tomatoes (including the juice).
6. Season with pepper and salt.
7. Bring to a boil, then reduce heat to low and simmer for 20-25 minutes until the sweet potatoes are tender and the lentils are cooked through.
8. Garnish with fresh cilantro, if desired.
9. Serve over brown rice or quinoa.

Nutrition Facts:

Per serving: Calories: 280 kcal, Carbs: 42 g, Proteins: 11 g, Fats: 7 g

Caprese Stuffed Portobello Mushrooms

Cooking Time: 15-20 mins   *Preparation Time: 15 mins*   *Servings: 2*

Ingredients:

- 4 large Portobello mushrooms
- 2 cups grape tomatoes, halved
- 1 cup fresh basil leaves, chopped
- 1 cup fresh mozzarella cheese, diced
- 2 tablespoons balsamic vinegar
- 2 tablespoons olive oil
- Pepper and salt to taste

Instructions:

1. Preheat the oven to 375°F (190°C).
2. Remove the stems from the Portobello mushrooms and clean the caps.
3. In a bowl, combine grape tomatoes, basil, mozzarella cheese, balsamic vinegar, olive oil, salt, and pepper.
4. Spoon the tomato mixture into the mushroom caps.
5. Place the stuffed mushrooms on a baking sheet and bake for 20-25 minutes until the mushrooms are tender and the cheese is melted.
6. Serve warm.

Nutrition Facts:
Per serving: Calories: 190 kcal, Carbs: 9 g, Proteins: 12 g, Fats: 12 g

Sweet Potato and Black Bean Chili

Cooking Time: 30-35 mins   *Preparation Time: 15 mins*   *Servings: 2*

Ingredients:

- 2 medium sweet potatoes, peeled and diced
- 1 can (15 ounces) of black beans, rinsed and drained
- 1 can (14 ounces) diced tomatoes
- 1 onion, diced
- 2 cloves garlic, minced
- 2 tablespoons chili powder
- 1 teaspoon ground cumin
- 1 teaspoon paprika
- 1 tablespoon olive oil
- Pepper and salt to taste
- Chopped fresh cilantro for garnish (optional)

Instructions:

1. Heat olive oil in a large pot over medium heat.
2. Add onion and garlic, and sauté until translucent.
3. Stir in chili powder, cumin, paprika, salt, and pepper. Cook for 1 minute.
4. Add diced sweet potatoes, black beans, and diced tomatoes (including the juice).
5. Bring to a boil, then reduce heat to low and simmer for 20-25 minutes until the sweet potatoes are tender.
6. Serve hot, garnished with chopped fresh cilantro if desired.

Nutrition Facts:

Per serving: Calories: 220 kcal, Carbs: 42 g, Proteins: 9 g, Fats: 4 g

Mediterranean Quinoa Salad

⌚ *Cooking Time: 15-20 mins*   🍳 *Preparation Time: 15 mins*   🍽 *Servings: 2*

Ingredients:

- *1 cup cooked quinoa*
- *1 cup cherry tomatoes, halved*
- *1 cup cucumber, diced*
- *1/2 cup Kalamata olives, pitted and halved*
- *1/4 cup diced red onion*
- *1/4 cup crumbled feta cheese*
- *2 tablespoons fresh lemon juice*
- *2 tablespoons olive oil*
- *1 tablespoon chopped fresh parsley*
- *Pepper and salt to taste*

Instructions:

1. In a large bowl, combine cooked quinoa, cherry tomatoes, cucumber, Kalamata olives, red onion, and feta cheese.
2. In a separate small bowl, whisk together lemon juice, olive oil, chopped parsley, salt, and pepper.
3. Pour the dressing over the quinoa mixture and toss well to combine.
4. Adjust pepper and salt according to taste.
5. Refrigerate for at least 30 minutes to allow the flavors to blend.
6. Serve chilled.

Nutrition Facts:

Per serving: Calories: 240 kcal, Carbs: 28 g, Proteins: 7 g, Fats: 12 g

Lentil and Vegetable Soup

⌚ *Cooking Time: 30-40 mins*   🍳 *Preparation Time: 15 mins*   🍽 *Servings: 2*

Ingredients:

- *1 cup dried green or brown lentils*
- *4 cups vegetable broth*
- *2 cups diced carrots*
- *2 cups diced celery*
- *1 onion, diced*
- *2 cloves garlic, minced*
- *1 can (14 ounces) diced tomatoes*
- *1 teaspoon dried thyme*
- *1 teaspoon dried oregano*
- *1 tablespoon olive oil*
- *Pepper and salt to taste*
- *Chopped fresh parsley for garnish (optional)*

Instructions:

1. Rinse the lentils under cold water.
2. In a large pot, heat olive oil over medium heat.
3. Add onion and garlic, and sauté until translucent.
4. Add diced carrots and celery. Cook for 5 minutes until slightly softened.
5. Stir in lentils, vegetable broth, diced tomatoes (including the juice), dried thyme, dried oregano, salt, and pepper.
6. Bring to a boil, then reduce heat to low and simmer for 25-30 minutes until the lentils and vegetables are tender.
7. Adjust pepper and salt according to taste.
8. Serve hot, garnished with chopped fresh parsley if desired.

Nutrition Facts:

Per serving: Calories: 220 kal, Carbs: 38g, Proteins: 12g, Fats: 3g

Spinach and Mushroom Quiche

⏱ *Cooking Time: 35-40 mins*   🍲 *Preparation Time: 20 mins*   🔔 *Servings: 2*

🧺 Ingredients:

- *1 pre-made whole wheat pie crust*
- *2 cups fresh spinach, chopped*
- *1 cup sliced mushrooms*
- *1/2 cup diced onion*
- *4 large eggs*
- *1 cup of low-fat milk*
- *1/2 cup shredded low-fat cheese*
- *1 tablespoon olive oil*
- *Pepper and salt to taste*

🥄 Instructions:

1. Preheat the oven to 375°F (190°C).
2. Heat olive oil in a skillet over medium heat.
3. Add diced onion and sliced mushrooms. Sauté until the mushrooms are tender.
4. Add chopped spinach to the skillet and cook until wilted.
5. In a bowl, whisk together eggs, milk, salt, and pepper.
6. Spread the sautéed vegetables evenly over the crust.
7. Pour the egg mixture over the vegetables.
8. Sprinkle shredded cheese on top.
9. Bake for 30-35 minutes until the quiche is set and golden brown.
10. Allow it to cool for a few minutes before slicing.
11. Serve warm or at room temperature.

Nutrition Facts:

Per serving: Calories: 250 kcal, Carbs: 20 g, Proteins: 12 g, Fats: 14 g

Chickpea and Vegetable Curry

⏱ *Cooking Time: 25-30 mins*   🍲 *Preparation Time: 15 mins*   🔔 *Servings: 2*

🧺 Ingredients:

- *1 can (15 ounces) chickpeas, rinsed and drained*
- *1 cup cauliflower florets*
- *1 cup diced bell peppers*
- *1 cup diced zucchini*
- *1 onion, diced*
- *2 cloves garlic, minced*
- *1 can (14 ounces) coconut milk (light option)*
- *1 can (14 ounces) diced tomatoes*
- *2 tablespoons curry powder*
- *1 tablespoon olive oil*
- *Pepper and salt to taste*
- *Chopped fresh cilantro for garnish (optional)*

🥄 Instructions:

1. Heat olive oil in a large pot over medium heat.
2. Add onion and garlic, and sauté until translucent.
3. Stir in curry powder, salt, and pepper. Cook for 1 minute.
4. Add cauliflower florets, diced bell peppers, and diced zucchini. Cook for 5 minutes until slightly softened.
5. Stir in chickpeas, coconut milk, and diced tomatoes (including the juice).
6. Bring to a boil, then reduce heat to low and simmer for 20-25 minutes until the vegetables are tender.
7. Adjust pepper and salt according to taste.
8. Serve hot, garnished with chopped fresh cilantro if desired.
9. Serve over brown rice or quinoa.

Nutrition Facts:

Per serving: Calories: 280 kcal, Carbs: 35 g, Proteins: 9 g, Fats: 12 g

Vibrant Green Carbonara

⌛ **Cooking Time:** 40-45 mins   🍲 **Preparation Time:** 20 mins   🛎 **Servings:** 2

🛒 Ingredients:

- ¾ tablespoon extra-virgin olive oil
- ¼ cup panko breadcrumbs, preferably whole-wheat
- 1 small clove garlic, minced
- 4 tablespoons grated Parmesan cheese, divided
- 1 ½ tablespoons finely chopped fresh parsley
- 2 large egg yolks
- 1 large egg
- ¼ teaspoon ground pepper
- ⅛ teaspoon salt
- 4.5 ounces fresh tagliatelle or linguine
- 4 cups baby spinach

📋 Instructions:

1. Bring 5 cups water to a boil in a large saucepan over high heat.
2. In the meantime, heat the oil in a large skillet over medium/high heat. Add the garlic and breadcrumbs and saute, stirring frequently, until browned, about 2 minutes. Transfer to a small bowl and stir in 1 tablespoon parmesan and parsley. Set aside.
3. In a medium bowl, whisk together remaining 3 tablespoons Parmesan, egg, egg yolks, pepper, and salt.
4. Add the pasta to the boiling water and cook for 1 minute, stirring occasionally. Add spinach and peas and cook until noodles are wilted, about 1 minute longer. Keep 1/4 cup water. Drain the pasta and transfer to a large bowl.
5. Whisking gently, add reserved cooking water to egg mixture. While tossing with tongs to combine, gradually add the mixture to the pasta.

Nutrition Facts:
Per serving: Calories: 430 kcal, Carbs: 54g, Proteins: 20g, Fats: 15

Veggie Stir-Fry with Tofu

⌛ **Cooking Time:** 15-20 mins   🍲 **Preparation Time:** 15 mins   🛎 **Servings:** 2

🛒 Ingredients:

- 1 package (14 ounces) of firm tofu, drained and cubed
- 2 cups mixed vegetables (broccoli florets, bell peppers, snap peas, carrots)
- 1 cup sliced mushrooms
- 1/2 cup sliced onions
- 2 cloves garlic, minced
- 2 tablespoons low-sodium soy sauce
- 1 tablespoon olive oil
- 1 teaspoon grated fresh ginger
- Pepper and salt to taste
- Chopped green onions for garnish (optional)

📋 Instructions:

1. Heat olive oil in a large skillet or wok over medium heat.
2. Add minced garlic and grated ginger. Sauté for 1 minute.
3. Add sliced onions and cook until slightly softened.
4. Add tofu cubes to the skillet and cook until lightly browned on all sides.
5. Add mixed vegetables and sliced mushrooms. Stir-fry for 5-7 minutes until the vegetables are crisp-tender.
6. Stir in low-sodium soy sauce, salt, and pepper. Cook for an additional 2 minutes.
7. Adjust pepper and salt according to taste.
8. Serve hot, garnished with chopped green onions if desired.
9. Serve over brown rice or quinoa.

Nutrition Facts:
Per serving: Calories: 220Kcal, Carbs: 15 g, Proteins: 16 g, Fats: 12 g

| The Diabetic Cookbook After 50

Putting Your Healthy Shopping List Together

Keep in mind that this is a strategy and a planned approach to eating a healthier diet. You must regard your shopping visits as missions, and your main goal should be to purchase the items on your list. No supplemental items, treats, or "just in case" purchases. You have to stay focused when you are shopping with a list.

Get a piece of paper or start a word processing file on your computer first. Your list will be incredibly straightforward and well-organized. To make your shopping trip easier, it is best to group the products you will be purchasing into general categories.

The sections to include on your shopping list are as follows:

1. Whole Grains: These are the grains found in your bread, pasta, and other grain-based foods. You won't be purchasing any goods made with white flour anymore. A healthy shopping list will include only 100% whole wheat or whole grain grains and cereals.

2. Fruits and veggies: All of the fruits and veggies you purchase will be fresh, and you will only purchase what you will require to last the upcoming few days. Vegetables left out for more than three to four days will spoil and must be thrown out. Don't throw your money away. The nutrients you get from fresh fruits and vegetables are worth the extra journey, even if you have to make it midweek.

3. Dairy Products: If you consume milk, you will likely purchase soy or skim milk. You should also include low-fat cheeses and yogurts in your list of dairy items. Even though dairy products shouldn't make up a large portion of a healthy shopping list, you should still include a few low-fat dairy items in your daily diet.

4. Meats & Poultry: Grease is not the word; disregard what you heard in the movie theater. The key word is LEAN! All of your meat cuts should be lean and nutritious. Choose round steaks rather than the well-liked strip steaks and T-bones. Choose ground turkey instead of ground beef. Finally, always make sure to purchase skinless chicken breasts when you go shopping.

The majority of your healthy shopping list should be composed of items from these four categories. Naturally, you'll also be buying other things like paper goods and cleaning supplies, but try to make at least one trip specifically for the foods on your healthy shopping list.

After separating the primary categories, you can make your own unique, healthy shopping list. Thanks to the categories, you can stay focused when you make your list. Just say no if you find yourself noticing a dish that doesn't fall under the categories mentioned above. The objective is to buy fresh, complete meals and stay away from unhealthy processed foods. In your effort to eat healthily, chips, cookies, and other junk food won't help you at all. Even if you don't have to give up sinful treats completely, try to stay away from them at the beginning of your healthy eating plan. Don't let a lot of unnecessary meals slow down your plans. It will be simpler to maintain a clean diet if your list is clean.

Prepare, set, and shop.
Set a goal for yourself to complete your shopping trip without making a single purchase that isn't on your list. You have created a healthy shopping list to ensure that you only purchase foods that will help you achieve your health and fitness goals. With a pen in hand, mark each item as it is added to the cart. Stay focused on collecting everything you need for the week and stick to your list until you leave the store.

One more tip for food shopping with a healthy list: Avoid going shopping while you are hungry. Those cookies look much more alluring when you're hungry rather than after eating something healthy. Eat something light because you might not feel like shopping if you're full from a hefty supper. A quick protein shot like Profect or Proasis is a smart choice for a meal before shopping. After consuming one of those, you won't feel hungry, and your body will be well-stocked with healthy protein to keep you alert, focused, and energized while shopping.

List Of Recipes in Alphabetical Order with Page Number

Avocado Toast with Poached Egg.......... 27
Apple Slices with Peanut Butter 36
Almond Flour Blueberry Muffins.......... 76
Baked Sweet Potato Fries................. 31
Baked Kale Chips........................ 33
Baked Zucchini Chips 35
Baked Parmesan Zucchini Fries 38
Baked Buffalo Cauliflower Bites 40
Baked Eggplant Chips.................... 39
Butternut Squash Soup 47
Baked Lemon Herb Salmon 52
Baked White Fish with Tomatoes and Olives. 54
Baked Lemon Dijon Tilapia 56
Blackened Cajun Shrimp Salad 58
Baked Dijon Salmon 59
Broiled Lemon Garlic Swordfish........... 59
Baked Parmesan Crusted Haddock........ 62
Black Bean and Vegetable Enchiladas.... 85
Caprese Skewers........................ 32
Cottage Cheese and Tomato Salad 33
Cucumber and Smoked Salmon Roll-Ups ... 37
Chicken Vegetable Soup 45
Chicken Tortilla Soup.................... 50
Chicken and Broccoli Stir-Fry............ 69
Chocolate Avocado Mousse 71
Coconut Chia Seed Popsicles 74
Chickpea Curry......................... 80
Caprese Stuffed Portobello Mushrooms..... 87
Chickpea and Vegetable Curry 89
Cauliflower Fried Rice 86
Cucumber Mint Cooler 77
Cinnamon Pear Crumble................. 73
Deviled Eggs 36
Eggplant Parmesan 80

Greek Yogurt Parfait 27
Guacamole with Veggie Slices............ 35
Greek Yogurt with Berries............... 31
Grilled Shrimp Skewers 52
Greek Salad............................ 46
Grilled Salmon with Avocado Salsa 54
Garlic and Herb Baked Shrimp........... 55
Grilled Lemon Herb Swordfish........... 56
Grilled Lemon Garlic Halibut............ 57
Greek Style Baked White Fish............ 61
Grilled Lemon Herb Chicken 65
Grilled Herb-Marinated Turkey Tenderloin 66
Grilled Teriyaki Chicken Stir-Fry......... 67
Grilled Balsamic Glazed Pork Chops 68
Greek Yogurt Parfait 73
Herb-Roasted Chicken Breast with Vegetables 66
Herb-Crusted Baked Chicken Thighs..... 68
Iced Green Tea with Lemon and Mint 75
Kale and Chickpea Soup 49
Lentil Soup............................ 43
Lemon Garlic Baked Salmon............. 53
Lemon Pepper Grilled Tuna Steaks 61
Low-Carb Berry Chia Pudding 72
Lentil and Vegetable Stir-Fry............ 79
Lentil and Vegetable Casserole 82
Lentil and Sweet Potato Curry........... 86
Lentil and Vegetable Soup............... 88
Mini Bell Pepper Nachos................ 40
Mixed Greens Salad with Grilled Chicken 43
Mexican Quinoa Salad.................. 49
Minestrone Soup 46
Mediterranean Quinoa Salad............ 88
Oven-Roasted Turkey Breast............. 67
Pesto Shrimp with Zucchini Noodles..... 62

The Diabetic Cookbook After 50 | 93

Pumpkin Spice Smoothie. 76
Quick Lemon-Blueberry Bites. 34
Quinoa and Vegetable Salad 45
Quinoa Stuffed Bell Peppers 81
Roasted Honeynut Squash. 41
Roasted Chickpeas 37
Roasted Beet and Orange Salad. 48
Spinach and Mushroom Breakfast Wrap 28
Spicy Roasted Edamame 39
Spinach and Berry Salad 44
Spinach and Feta Soup. 48
Seared Scallops with Cauliflower Mash. 55
Steamed Asian Ginger White Fish 57
Shrimp and Avocado Salad 63
Sugar-Free Apple Crisp 71
Sugar-Free Banana Bread. 72
Sparkling Berry Infused Water 75
Sugar-Free Coconut Macaroons 74
Spinach and Chickpea Curry 83
Sweet Potato and Black Bean Chili 87
Spinach and Mushroom Quiche 89
Spinach and Feta Stuffed Portobello Mushrooms . .84
Turkey Lettuce Wraps 38
Tomato Basil Soup. 44
Tuna Salad with Avocado .47
Tuna Salad Lettuce Wraps 53
Thai Coconut Curry Shrimp 60
Turkey Meatballs with Zucchini Noodles. 65
Tofu and Vegetable Stir-Fry. 84
Veggie Omelet 28
Veggie Sticks with Hummus 32
Vibrant Green Carbonara .90
Veggie Stir-Fry with Tofu .90
Vegetable Stir-Fry. 79
Whole Grain Pancakes. 29
Zucchini Noodles with Tomato and Basil 85

Cooking Conversion Chart

TEMPERATURES EQUIVALENTS	
FAHRENHEIT (°F)	CELSIUS (°C)
225	107
250	120
275	135
300	150
325	160
350	180
375	190
400	205
425	220
450	235
475	245
500	260

WEIGHT EQUIVALENTS	
US STANDARD	METRIC (g)
1 oz	28
2 oz	57
5 oz	142
10 oz	284
15 oz	425
16 oz (1 pound)	455
1.5 pounds	680
2 pounds	907

VOLUME EQUIVALENTS (LIQUID)		
US STANDARD	US STANDARD (OUNCES)	METRIC APPROXIMATE)
1 teaspoon	0.17 fl.oz.	5 mL
1 tablespoon	0.5 fl.oz.	15 mL
2 tablespoons	1 fl.oz.	30 mL
1/4 cup	2 fl.oz	60 mL
1/2 cup	4 fl.oz	120 mL
1 cup	8 fl.oz	240 mL
1 1/2 cup	12 fl.oz	355 mL
2 cups or 1 pint	16 fl.oz	475 mL
4 cups or 1 quart	33 fl.oz	0.95 L
1 gallon	128 fl.oz	3.78 L

US STANDARD			METRIC
3 teaspoons	1 tablespoon	1/2 ounce	14 g
2 tablespoons	1/8 cup	1 ounce	28 g
4 tablespoons	1/4 cup	2 ounces	57 g
8 tablespoons	1/2 cup	4 ounces	114 g
12 tablespoons	3/4 cup	6 ounces	170 g
16 tablespoons	1 cup	8 ounces	227 g
32 tablespoons	2 cups	16 ounces (1 pound)	455 g

VOLUME EQUIVALENTS (SOLID)	
US STANDARD	METRIC
1/8 teaspoon	0.5 mL
1/4 teaspoon	1 mL
1/2 teaspoon	2 mL
3/4 teaspoon	4 mL
1 teaspoon	5 mL
1 tablespoon	15 mL
1/4 cup	59 mL
1/2 cup	118 mL
3/4 cup	177 mL
1 cup	235 mL
2 cups	475 mL

REFERENCES

- "Glycemic Index and Diabetes: MedlinePlus Medical Encyclopedia." Glycemic Index and Diabetes: MedlinePlus Medical Encyclopedia, medlineplus.gov/ency/patientinstructions/000941.htm.

- American Diabetes Association (www.diabetes.org)

- American Diabetes Association. (2019). Standards of Medical Care in Diabetes—2019 Abridged for Primary Care Providers. Clinical Diabetes, 37(1), 11-34.

- National Institute of Diabetes and Digestive and Kidney Diseases (www.niddk.nih.gov)

Printed in Great Britain
by Amazon